The Men in My Country

sightline books

The Iowa Series in Literary Nonfiction

Patricia Hampl & Carl H. Klaus, series editors

Marilyn Abildskov
The Men in My Country

University of Iowa Press, Iowa City

University of Iowa Press, Iowa City 52242

Copyright © 2004 by Marilyn Abildskov

All rights reserved

Printed in the United States of America

Design by Richard Hendel

www.uiowapress.org

The events described here are real. Some characters
have been given fictitious names and identifying
characteristics in order to protect their anonymity.

Portions of this book appeared in different form
in the following literary magazines: *Apalachee Review*,
Drunken Boat, *Fourth Genre*, *Puerto del Sol*, *Quarterly West*,
and *Sonora Review*.

Printed on acid-free paper

Library of Congress
Cataloging-in-Publication Data
Abildskov, Marilyn, 1961–.
The men in my country / Marilyn Abildskov.
p.   cm.—(Sightline books)
ISBN 978-1-58729-449-5 (pbk)
1. Japan—Description and travel.   2. Abildskov,
Marilyn, 1961– —Travel—Japan.   3. Americans—
Japan.   I. Title.   II. Series.
DS812.A25   2004
952.04´9´08691—dc22   2004046076

Which of the young men does she like the best?
Ah the homeliest of them is beautiful to her.
—WALT WHITMAN

For beyond the difficulty of articulating yourself in the
world there remains the difficulty of being yourself.
—VIRGINIA WOOLF

How lush the world is,
how full of things that don't belong to me—
—LOUISE GLÜCK

The Men in My Country

t starts as a name, a place, a squiggle on a map. *Japan.* A country as far away from familiar as familiar can be. I try to imagine the country, what its streets look like, how its air smells. I touch the country on a map, fingering the page of a weathered atlas, spine broken, yellowed pages flying apart. As big as a thumbprint, as small as a canoe. *Japan.* I like the sound of it.

When my best friend called to say there was a job in Japan, when she asked, did I want to go, I knew I would. I would say yes, I would sign a contract to take me to Japan for the year. The job? To teach at three different junior highs. The town? A medium-sized city in the mountains, someplace called Matsumoto. I had just turned thirty, a watershed year. I would start over that year. I knew I would. I wanted to, I needed to. I didn't know the difference then between want and need. All I knew is that I had to get away and when I stared at my name on the Japanese contract, the squiggles of *katakana*, my name typed in English sturdily beneath, I liked how it looked. As if it—as if *I*—were translated, transformed, emerging now as someone new.

And within a month, I had arrived. Sleeping on *tatami* mats. Eating rice. Washing blue-and-white bowls. Hanging laundry out on the balcony to dry. I loved the smell of sun-dried shirts and cotton sweaters that carried a hint of wind and earth. A new wind. A new earth.

I loved attending to errands that used to be mundane. Going to the post office. The stationery shop. The video store. Shopping at the Apple supermarket with its tofu, its persimmons, its miso, its multiplicity of squid. I'd think how strange it is to be in one place one day, another the next; how strange it is that one day you're unhappy, the next day you're not. Before I came to Japan, I woke up crying in the morning as if I had some virus I could never quite shake. Once I arrived, I woke up eager to get out and look around again. And for that, I thanked the place.

The place. Here was a place where whole holidays were devoted to looking, just looking. At first I thought there was something a little slow in that, a little *odd* maybe, a little *dull*, just watching cherry blossoms blossom or fireflies fly or looking at the light of moon. But once I lived in Japan a while, once I started to fall into a rhythm of the weeks and the days, one calendar year soon slid into two, and I came to love what comes from watching with care. I came to cherish in an ordinary day how much an ordinary person could see.

The woman at the post office figuring change out on an abacus, *click, click, click.* The men outside workplaces doing jumping jacks. The girls walking from *juku*, black braids swinging, bodies wrapped in dark crow-like coats. There were the boys who rode their bikes to kendo class, swords strapped to their small, boyish backs. Swords on boys — such an achingly archaic sight.

I watched, I listened, I took it all in. For a long time, this was the pleasure, the thrill. To learn the body of Japan, the curve of its rivers, the bright red of its Shinto shrines, the sound of its ambulances, dissonant and slow. To know the country sensually and to love it through its bamboo trees, its *ramen*, its sweet-bean pastries, its *sentō* and *onsen.*

I reveled in this way of knowing Japan, of moving through streets like an animal or child, pointing and speaking in simple words. *Train station — where? Bread — how much? Hot today? Yes! Atsui ne!* I was pleased to learn these simple words, pleased to learn the country's etiquette. I liked learning to receive each gift graciously, be it cookies or pears or a small handkerchief, always with two hands, not one, and bowing, bowing low. I watched, mesmerized, as shop owners in china shops wrapped each blue-and-white dish, these dishes I bought to make myself a home. Just one or two at a time. A plate here. A pair of rice bowls there. A square serving dish for sushi I took home and used for serving everything from green salad to potato chips. The woman at the shop, one of many with luminous skin, packed each dish in tissue paper first, then newspaper after that, placing each carefully wrapped dish within a box, a box I would nestle in the large basket on the front of my bike, riding home more slowly than usual so no dish would break.

When friends back home asked why I chose to stay in Japan, I said I loved the dishes. Not the food, though I loved the food too, but the actual *dishes*, the breakable porcelain kind. I loved the pencil boxes too, loved living in a place where people carried writing supplies in small, tidy bundles made of straw or metal or plastic or wood. I loved seeing vendors selling hot chestnuts on the street. The feel of *tatami* mats under my feet. The faint smell of cedar as I fell asleep. I told my friends back home, I loved living life lower, loved sleeping on the floor. On pillows filled with beans. Waking to light seeping through delicate *shōji*, those perfect sliding paper-thin doors.

One Saturday two boys came to repair my torn paper doors. They arrived at my apartment wearing Levi's and t-shirts under soft flannel shirts. A jolt went through me. I'd not seen them out of their standard-issue school uniforms, those stiff dark pants and gold-buttoned coats, the military kind with collars that cut at the throat. And so, as they stood there in the *genkan*, taking off their boots and coats, revealing what they wore underneath, I looked at them and some mad mix of desire ran through me, a force teetering between maternal desire and something else.

Oh, I thought, as the afternoon of repairs began. The backdrop changes *everything*. The boys did not look like boys anymore.

The next Monday at school, a girl showed up at my desk in the teachers' room and stood so close that I could smell her, a mix of warm milk and cold rice and the moist beginnings of adolescent sweat, and she said nothing as she produced thin *origami* sheets from her book bag and then, with fingers as stubby as crayons, folded a paper family for me.

A blue kangaroo mother.

A yellow bird of a father.

And a small neon green box, for which she used an English word. *Baby*.

I repeated after her. *Baby*.

Then the girl floated away and I never saw her again.

I loved Japan, I truly did. But there I was, an American woman living in Japan, turning thirty-one and then thirty-two, and I knew that no matter how much I felt a part of the place, I, too, could float away, that no one would notice, that I would not leave a trace. I watched the place from a distance; that distance made me ache.

In coffee shops couples sat with one another, eyes closed. At bus stops young women buried their noses in books whose titles were covered in brown paper wraps. At construction sites, men nodded gravely as I pedaled by. I would smile or wave, knowing I would unsettle the devil out of them if I dared to stop. No one touched me. No one ever looked me in the eye.

And so the place remained foreign, its secret lives a secret to me. And the body is not the mind, after all. And a country is more than a sum of its sensory parts. And so, I wanted to go deeper, I wanted to go inside the country's mind, I wanted the country under my skin.

Which is why, when I think of it now, nearly a decade later, when I think of all that happened at the end, I think I must have been ripe for trouble. I must have been ready to meet those three men.

meet Nozaki through conversation class. I meet him long before I meet the other men, long before the trouble at the end
begins. For a long time, Nozaki means very little to me. He is
just another face in the crowd of Japanese businessmen.

On the third floor of a crumbling building the businessmen
gather once a month for "free conversation" in English with
me, their teacher, a native speaker. This back-and-forth dia-
logue, their leader, Mr. Yoshida, explains, will not require a textbook
and anyway, free conversation will encourage a more meaningful "cultural exchange."

At first I am charmed by this, at what "cultural exchange" here
means: that the businessmen will crack jokes most nights in Japanese — jokes about each other, each other's wives, each other's girlfriends, real and pretend; jokes about waistlines that thicken, jokes
about hair as it thins. Their jokes, I reason, give me a glimpse into a
part of Japan I would otherwise miss; their jokes, I figure, give me a
glimpse into the *real* foreign country to a woman like me — the real
world of men.

For a long time, then, I overlook the fact that we meet in a room
with windows so grungy they refuse to open and doors so warped they
refuse to close. I overlook the thick fog of smoke that envelops us, the
way the smoke stings my sensitive nose. I overlook the fact that the
businessmen are the worst students ever, most of them arriving late
or leaving early, never trying to speak a word of English. Instead I
revel in what seems all in good fun, teaching the men about American customs, about smoking and non-smoking sections in American
restaurants, listening as they respond to this, saying it is shocking to
think there are places a man cannot smoke, that this, Miss Marilyn,
is a reason to live in Japan. I overlook a lot and appreciate that the

men are not children like my students in junior high. And I know, they overlook a lot about me, my own long list of failings — the fact, for instance, that I have no idea how to teach; the fact, for instance, that after all this time, I still speak only the most simple and halting Japanese. We overlook the trouble and instead take pleasure in making each other laugh.

One night, when no one has done the homework assigned the month before, and each has admitted that, in fact, no, he hadn't remembered there *was* any homework to do, I write the classic American excuse on the blackboard: *My dog ate my homework.* Mr. Kato nods his head vigorously to suggest he understands, and then blurts out, *My wife ate my homework!* which gets him a big laugh from the others in the room.

Then he adds: *My wife are a goat!*

On another night the businessmen beg me to teach them swear words in English, which I do out of a sense of duty as well as sport, introducing the phrase *fuck you* as an insult, the way I taught them last month, in a lesson on restaurant English, *Do you have a smoking section here?*

But the concept of *fuck you* as crude insult escapes them all, goes right over their heads.

Sex, it is GOOD, Mr. Yoshida says, his expression perplexed. He has failed to grasp how an invitation for sex might be considered rude.

You have a point, I say, making a mental note to save the nuances of *motherfucker* as a term of endearment for another day.

I give up trying to cure them of asking the question they so often ask, *Do you like play sex?* and instead take another approach, urging them to add one small word to make the question slightly more grammatically correct. *Do you like TO play sex?* I suggest, because the verb *to play* seems better and more sensual than the acquisitive verb *to have*. And I love them for making me think about the grammar of sex.

The months come, the months go.

Then the romance begins to lose its shine, the adoration begins to fade. We start to get on each other's nerves. Charm turns slowly toward tedium. That they smoke during class begins to make me feel ill. Will we go down in flames together? I think, *I cannot think of a worse way to go.*

Now when they make jokes I begin to think they are joking about *me*, saying that Miss Marilyn is unlucky or why else would she be thirty years old and then thirty-one and living in this, a foreign country, all by herself? Does she not have any marriage prospects?

I up the ante, try to make our lessons more substantial somehow, turning this into a more serious *English* class. I come to class with handouts and photocopies of articles from the *Japan Times*. I come prepared to pose questions about the latest bribery scandal out of Tokyo, or Japan's mix of high consumer prices and low unemployment, or the contours of Japanese royalty as Princess Masako marries out of a sense of duty to country, the newspapers say, not just loyalty or love of an individual man. And what do the Japanese businessmen do? They doze off, their sleepy eyes getting more sleepy all the time. And as they do, I start zoning out too, wondering what on earth possessed me to think that bribery or capitalism or the nature of royalty was worth discussion, worth any discussion at all.

Only two subjects bring them back to life, only two subjects animate them. Sex. And golf. Two subjects about which I know little and nothing.

You are my boon and my bane, I say one night as they chat amiably among themselves about their last golf game together, a discussion that makes me feel guilty for accepting money to supposedly teach.

What is boon? Mr. Yoshida asks. *And bane, what is that?*

I shake my head. Shrug my shoulders. I am a bad teacher, using clichés and idioms at the drop of a hat. Idioms and jokes — the hardest parts of language to penetrate.

Let's just say, I continue, *we are a bad match*. Plaid and polka dots.

One night the businessmen slump forward, cigarettes dangling from outstretched arms. They yawn, they smile, they close their eyes. I have asked a series of questions about abstract art. It's a bust, a total bust. So I scrap the lesson and suggest we play a little game.

Would you rather do *this* or *that*? Be *that* or *this*? Swim or ski? Make public policy or plant trees? Be rich or happy?

Nozaki says he would rather sleep than drink, would rather drink than eat, and would rather think than play *pachinko* or anything else.

Mr. Yoshida says he would rather play sex in the kitchen than in the living room.

Mr. Kato says he would rather play sex right here.

The lesson continues. I can't wait to leave. I don't understand it—how what used to amuse has lost its sheen.

The days continue, the routine plods along. At Meizen Junior High, I run through the activities meant to make language come alive, walking up and down the aisles of each class, mimicking animal sounds in English.

What does a duck say? Quack, quack, quack! *What does a cat say?* Meow! Meow!

The children marvel. How can a duck say anything but *gaa-gaa?* Doesn't Miss Marilyn know a cat says *nya-nya?*

The English teacher in Japan: a well-paid monkey, a friend of mine says. Read and repeat. Read and repeat. Tape recorders come alive.

I met a woman once who, on a trip to Moscow, visited Pavlov's lab. Pavlov was dead at the time but the dog—which is many dogs, not one, like Lassie, she said—lived and dutifully endured various experiments.

What did the dogs look like? I asked.

The dogs looked tired, the woman said.

For the businessmen, I plan a lesson on writing love letters, thinking love letters will let them speak of their mistresses and private lives without fear. But the businessmen give up on sex; the lesson leans into tenderness. The businessmen become dutiful students, listening quietly to the CD I have brought, a duet by Willie Nelson and Johnny Cash, full of phrases I say might be of use: *always on my mind* and *crazy for you* and *I still miss someone*. And then they work on their letters, looking up words in earnestness in their dictionaries—*respect, kindness, admiration, adore*—and writing these words out in careful script.

Mr. Mori writes, *You are the woman I admire more than anyone in world*, and tells us he is writing to his mother and that his letter is *an honest, no lie*.

Mr. Yoshida reads his letter out loud but refuses to tell us as a group who the letter is addressed to. Then after class, he whispers that Mr. Yoshida's letter is not for his Thai mistress as perhaps Miss Marilyn suspects. His letter, he says, is for a girl he admired from afar in seventh grade.

Then the next month, the conversation veers back to sex and golf.

One night Mr. Kato says he very much likes to play with himself. Golf, he means. I stifle a smile. I know he means BY himself, not WITH himself. The routine is back on track, its rhythm sure. They're back in the groove, the businessmen, talking about sex and golf, golf and sex. I give up trying to talk them out of this.

I give up on all but one.

One intrigues me. Not all at once, but over time. He doesn't show up for the night of writing love letters. He doesn't come but half the time. For a long time, I don't even know his name. Then one night in class this man says something about John Updike's novel, *Couples*, the story of ten couples in a small New England town.

The conversation floats around sex and marriage throughout the night. I have tried to harness that energy by writing on the blackboard the word *infidelity*.

Then this man asks point-blank if I have read Updike's novel and I lie, saying yes. This should be a sign, of course: that we lie to the ones who matter most.

But it's too early for signs, too early to say what matters most. Right now he's still just some guy in the class of Japanese businessmen and there is some charged quality, some crackle, some snap, some spit, something that makes me sit up straight and pay attention. Attention as the first sign of love to come. And in that quality of attention is something I recognize and miss.

And then?

As everyone begins to leave and I am gathering up my things, he turns and looks at me and holds the look just one beat too long. He smiles. Then leaves.

The gesture is thrilling, the gesture is understood: Here in a country where it's rude to look someone directly in the eye, he has done exactly that. He has made a move. Stared at me. I understand now a certain phrase, its weight, its wonder. *He fixed his gaze.*

Later that night, I rumble around in my files to pull out my notes: a cheat sheet that offers the barest of facts, facts that will later lean into story.

Hiro Nozaki. That is his name.

A lawyer. From Shiojiri. But he spent the bulk of his adulthood in Tokyo instead of this small town of Shiojiri where the others have always lived. And this. *Single*. This is the word I have written down many months before. *Single*. A word that I hate, a word that has always seemed to me a caricature of the more elegant word, *alone*. Yet this is what I've written. *Single*. A word that now shimmers with possibility, with heat.

I think of how Nozaki enters a room, walking slowly, more leisurely than the rest. I think of how Nozaki smokes a cigarette, savoring it to the very end. I think of how he looks some nights: so tired, so handsome. Sometimes he looks like he's been dragged through an oil slick. Sometimes he looks like a 1940s movie star, the kind of man who could pull off wearing pleated pants. Neglected. Elegant. There's some basic contradiction in him that appeals to my contradictory-loving head.

I think of how little I know of Nozaki. But what I know I know. That look, that smile, that quality of the air. I make a mental note that the two of us must find a way to get together outside of class.

But we don't meet. Not outside of class, anyway. Not that first year or second. We go out for *ramen* sometimes, sure. We share a few beers. But it's always with the others, in the presence of the group of Japanese businessmen.

At each of these gatherings, it is Nozaki I watch, Nozaki I hope to be seated near. But the rules in Japan are bigger than me. And so, one night, after class, when we go out as a group for yakitori and beer, Mr. Yoshida tells me, Miss Marilyn must sit next to him, for custom in Japan means the teacher must sit next to the most senior member of the group. I nod my head. Make small talk now. Does Mr. Yoshida prefer chopsticks to forks? Bread to rice? Sapporo to Kirin beer?

Mr. Yoshida's attention drifts elsewhere, down the row. He is as bored with me as I am with him. Nozaki, at the end of the table, says something and the whole group explodes. I feel a surge of pride at his cleverness, his wit. He has told a joke. Nozaki has told a joke tonight.

What did he say? I ask Mr. Yoshida. *What did Mr. Nozaki say just now?* I crave translation of this amazing night. I try to sound casual as if interested in the portal of light this joke might offer on the culture as a whole. But I am far from casual. I am intent on knowing what he just said.

Mr. Yoshida hesitates. *It is very difficult to say.*

But won't you try?

He turns to Mr. Kato and the two whisper for a while, then Mr. Yoshida turns back and says, *It is too — what is the word in English? Complex.* Nozaki's joke, it seems, used word play in Japanese.

Of course, I think. Of course Nozaki would tell a sophisticated joke. I think of something I read in a book years before: that a joke offers consolation of sorts.

Then Mr. Yoshida says the thing we both know will hurt, that I also deserve.

Miss Marilyn needs to study Japanese.

I invite the businessmen to my apartment one night to watch the movie *Planes, Trains and Automobiles,* reasoning that we can combine a social event with some practical travel English, phrases that these business-men, many of whom travel to English-speaking countries, might use.

Where is the gate to Flight Number 2931?

What time does the next bus leave?

Can you tell me where to get a taxi, please?

But underneath these stated reasons, I am hoping that Nozaki will come, too, and that after he does, he will have my address and after that, he will want to drop in. And after that? Maybe he will compli-ment Marilyn-san on being so neat. Or become so comfortable that he opens my refrigerator looking for something to eat. I imagine him looking through a stack of CDs and pulling out all the sad country songs and saying he likes sad country songs and I am liking that be-cause I cannot imagine being with someone who doesn't love country music, its hard-won simplicity, its happiness and sadness all mixed.

But Nozaki doesn't show up that night. Instead, the others arrive and all at once, my apartment is filled with black-haired businessmen, each of whom is carrying food: a bucket of Kentucky Fried Chicken; large bags of potato chips; liters of pop, all of which the businessmen proceed to eat and drink with great gusto along with the meal I had prepared for us in advance — a large bowl of pasta salad and warm slices of buttered sourdough bread. Within minutes, all the food — theirs and mine — is gone and I see that my meal was too slight for us and the businessmen knew this, they must have known. And before the movie even begins, I wonder, how did they know this? How did they know I would fail to anticipate their hunger?

What I learn of Nozaki as the months go by could fill a teacup drop by drop. That he doesn't like golf. That he drives an old car. That he quotes French films instead of action flicks.

He's not like the others.

He's not like the rest.

I find myself thinking this each time he shows up at class. One month he's there, the next month he's not.

He's not like the other businessmen. Because so far he has resisted *omiai*. The other businessmen find this strange, I can tell, and ask him one night, *what's THAT about? Why NOT agree to an arranged marriage?* After all, Nozaki-san is not a young man anymore. He is thirty-seven years old. What is Nozaki-san waiting for?

Even I have to admit that the custom sounds harmless enough, suspiciously similar to a blind date in the West, albeit a highly ritualized blind date, one where the families of the two people gather for dinner as the two unmarried people check each other out. What would it hurt to agree to meet a woman some matchmaker found? In the old days, only the man could refuse a second date, but now in contemporary Japan, after an initial meeting, either party can opt to back out.

But Nozaki holds his ground and refuses, saying he prefers to wait to find the right woman on his own, that he believes too much in the natural course of love.

I leave class wondering what the natural course of love is.

One night in class, I ask the businessmen to name one Japanese person they truly admire. As an example, I mention the historian who has been in the news, someone who has spent his lifetime working for the Japanese Education Ministry to revise textbooks to be fairer in their treatment of World War II.

Most choose sports figures I cannot pretend to have heard of before. Mr. Yamaguchi chooses his mother. Nozaki chooses a character from the French film, *The Big Blue*. Mr. Kato says, *Miss Marilyn because she came to Japan one person, no family and even if she gets homesick, she stays.*

I write the word "flattery" on the blackboard but Mr. Kato continues, *No I am not flattery. It is true, it is true.*

It doesn't matter, really. Mr. Kato just rubs me exactly the wrong way.

When class ends, it's Mr. Kato who offers to drive me to the train station. When we reach his car, I see it is a tiny red convertible, one so small I am afraid I won't be able to squeeze the whole of my body in.

This is my wife's car, he says.

Oh, lucky her, I say. *It's very smart.*

But I use it to go Tokyo every weekend to see my girlfriends.

This is the kind of thing Mr. Kato says routinely in class. I twist my legs so my feet aren't on top of my bag. The car's so small I feel I ought to hold my breath.

Mr. Kato flips a switch on the front dashboard and a CD — Japanese pop music, tinny and loud — comes on. It's like a spaceship, this car. So many gadgets.

I have LOTS of girlfriends, Mr. Kato says, putting his hand directly on my thigh. *I wasn't flattery tonight, Miss Marilyn.*

And in a moment of clarity — and in a moment that will seem ironic soon enough — I remove Mr. Kato's hand from my thigh and look him in the eyes, hoping he will understand the gesture as rude, before saying, *I do not want to hear about your affairs.*

Then I spill out of the car and run to the train, feeling ridiculous, wondering why Nozaki couldn't be the one to give me a lift, why it couldn't have been Nozaki tonight placing his hand on my thigh.

Nozaki, the mystery man. That's what Natsume-san, owner of the ABC School, will say a few months from now when I ask if she knows anything about him, about this one businessman. *No,* she will tell me, *but I will ask around town.* And then? What does she find? *Nothing,* she says. *He is the mystery.*

O ne night in class Nozaki says that culture is one thing, but not the only thing; that he is Japanese culturally and always will be, which is fine, but that his mind is wide, is not bound by nationality.

Has Nozaki ever traveled? I ask. *Ever wanted to see other parts of the world?*

I can feel the eyes of the other businessmen on us both, wondering at the meaning behind Marilyn-*sensei's* singular approach. No one is laughing tonight; no one is making any golf- or sex-related jokes.

In one way, no, Nozaki says. But in another way, he has already traveled the globe.

What do you mean? I ask.

And in an answer that confirms everything I will come to love, he says: *I read.*

meet the second man through Ken'ichi, a ninth-grade student at Meizen Junior High. Ken'ichi won the school's, then the city's annual English speech contest in the fall and now, in January, he is going on to compete at the next level in Nagano-ken.

Miss Kita and I take the train from Matsumoto to Nagano City where we sit in a cold high school auditorium, listening to one speech after another, waiting for our student, Ken'ichi's turn. We have worked with him for weeks leading up to this event, helped him practice his "r's"—notoriously difficult for Japanese tongues—and urged him to show a little enthusiasm when he speaks.

But maybe keep your hands still? I suggest. The trick at these speech contests is to achieve balance, to avoid looking stiff but by the same token, to avoid looking overly needy, like a theatrical freak.

At Meizen the classrooms look all alike. Old hardwood floors. Beat-up desks, six across, six deep. Potted flowers near a sink. And a blackboard that students, including Ken'ichi, wash twice a day during our ritual cleaning shifts. Outside is a garden filled with snow all winter and flowers all spring.

What are these? I asked my colleagues once, the Japanese English teachers who want me to help them practice their speaking skills. I pointed to a dark red flower in Meizen's garden that I had never seen anywhere in the United States. It looked like a more vivid version of an Indian paintbrush.

Muzukashii, muzukashii, the teachers said. Translations are difficult. They shuffled around in their dictionaries, opened up the pages of gardening books but no one knew, no one could say. I looked at the flowers just beginning to blossom that spring and wondered if it is the naming of something that makes it real or the mystery of not knowing that makes it memorable instead.

The contest continues and the contestants continue, one by one, when finally it's Ken'ichi's turn, Ken'ichi who is bouncing happily onto the stage. But before he opens his mouth, Miss Kita and I can tell he's doomed. He looks frightened — like a cat I knew who loomed large in its house, overshadowing its owner in every important way but outside was vulnerable, a small jewel on the doorstep, shrinking against a darkening orange sky.

I want to judges thank, Ken'ichi begins, *for listening me to in some for advance. I am today pleasing this speech to give.*

My chest constricts. He is not reading the words on the page, the ones Miss Kita and I spent weeks helping him smooth out and organize. He is trying to speak from the heart. But the heart is riddled with error upon error. The heart makes no grammatical sense. The heart has only flashes of linguistic flair.

Ken'ichi will not take home a ribbon for first or second or even third. He will not place. Of that I am sure. I am already composing the speech I will give to him Monday morning when, sad-faced, he returns to school. But for now I am trying to smile supportively and pretend that I hear nothing wrong since Ken'ichi, hands flying about his face unnaturally, seems to be looking directly at me.

And so, he continues, refusing to look down at his carefully constructed notes, forgetting everything he practiced toward, *Begin let me. To speech about Japan most valuable issue: littering.*

After the speeches, while the judges tally their scores behind closed doors, the rest of us move to the teachers' room for cookies and tea.

Anyway, Miss Kita says, excusing herself, *I must go to bathroom now.* And I realize I have been a terrible colleague to her, rarely if ever correcting her mistakes and imprinting her with my own inarticulate ways. I say "anyway," for instance, to change subjects sometimes and now I have become aware that Miss Kita has started doing the same.

The idea of correcting someone else's mistakes, which I'm told is a part of my job as assistant English teacher, makes me shudder, partly because there is so much about English I don't know. Split infinitives and past perfect and participles and gerunds — these parts of formal grammar remain a foreign language to me. The first time a Japanese English teacher asked, *explain to me gerund*, I thought she was asking about Gerald, another American English teacher in town, and I said I knew him vaguely, not particularly well, but he seemed like a good guy, kind and gentle, *yasashii*.

Once, a Japanese English teacher at Kasei asked that I be more aggressive in teaching her more natural ways to speak, and so, to comply, I told her that perhaps a more common way of saying *Oh, what a pity* is *That's too bad*, and she began saying that—*That's too bad!*—so much that afterward I felt pained and went around for days with the phrase *Oh, what a pity* bouncing around in my head like a pinball, liking it, missing it, wondering if others who taught English suffered this kind of small anxiety attack, concern over the strange and beautiful and unanswerable intricacies of language, the price of turning *pity* into something *too bad*.

I'm thinking about all that, about how funny language is, how much gets lost in translation, when a Japanese woman with a face like a cow appears and says, *I used to think you smelled like butter when I was a child.*

At first I think she's talking about *me*, saying *I* smell like butter and I have half a mind to apologize and to sniff at my armpit to see if maybe she's right.

Instead, I stare and stare and wonder if it's true. *Do* I smell like butter? Does she have a point? Then something clicks and I can hear: she means Americans *generally*, not specifically *me*.

Did you? I say.

She nods vigorously.

I take note of her face, which is so anonymous and ordinary that its very lack of distinction surprises me. When I first arrived in this country, the women looked so uniformly beautiful, each one thin with shiny, thick dark hair, each one more exquisite than the last, that I couldn't help but balk at all that female beauty, sneer at the sheer excess of it.

But then, after a few months, the novelty wore off and a cruel clarity revealed itself, one that suggested women here were like women anywhere, some blessed with beauty, some, like this woman standing here, blessed with faces like mine. Ordinary. Anonymous. A face you would never remember from a crowd.

Face. In Japanese the word is *kao*, pronounced *cow*.

We should become friends, I thought, staring at this woman. Because we both have *kaos*.

But we won't become friends. The obvious pairings never occur.

Right then an American woman named Natalie, whom I know in passing, interrupts. She's one of a few dozen other Americans I know from around Nagano-ken. She used to hang out at Scotty's, Matsumoto's best expatriate bar because it is the town's *only* expatriate bar. Natalie's here tonight to listen to one of her Japanese students as well, a seventh-grader named Miyuki, whose speech, I could tell, dazzled everyone.

Miyuki gave a speech about the tension in Japan over importing foreign rice, how the reluctance to accept foreign influence was understandable, maybe even good. After all, so many Japanese people, she'd said, remember what it was like during World War II to go hungry, to feel that pit in the bottom of their empty stomachs, to miss the taste of a full meal of rice and fish or the luxury afterward of a small square of chocolate, bitter and strong. They knew what it was like to go without. And so, it was natural for Japanese people to want to be self-sufficient, to avoid relying on foreign-grown food. But, she said, isolation would only hurt Japan in the long run.

Your student's speech was terrific, I say. And I mean it. Miyuki was poised and sophisticated, her presentation flawless, her pronunciation sound.

Thanks, Natalie says. *She's a true perfectionist. And she thrives under pressure.*

I'm amazed by that and feel a rush of tenderness for poor Ken'ichi and the rest of us who, like him, buckle under pressure. I pray that somehow Ken'ichi will not realize how poorly he's done.

Then Natalie touches my arm, says there's someone I should meet, and she introduces me to a Japanese man. Salt and pepper hair. Stocky build.

A professor, she says, *of sociology here in town. A student in my night class at the Let's Talk! conversation school.*

I turn. Smile. Extend my buttery American hand.

The professor smiles and bows.

He is middle-aged, somewhere between thirty-nine and fifty-five. His face reminds me of a window, open wide. He is smiling and I am remembering how, when I first arrived, I smiled openly in every photograph taken of teachers at school until finally someone corrected me, telling me that to smile in a photograph in Japan is to reveal one-self as a lunatic.

I smile at the professor. I am a lunatic. The professor smiles back. His smile reveals very nice, sane-looking teeth. The cow-woman wanders off. Then names are traded, pleasantries exchanged. The talk is generic, centering on the speech contest we have just heard.

Did you like the speech about littering in Japan?

Wasn't the girl in red relaxed?

What about the speech railing against conformity?

The professor's English is perfect. There are no participles dangling like unsightly bits of dry rice stuck to a chin. Perfect English. Clean and correct. I have lived here long enough to know how rare it is to hear someone speak like that. There is something stirring in this, the correctness of the professor's speech, as if I am watching a fragile house of cards go up and now must watch to see if or when it will fall.

I take note of particulars: blue suit, white shirt, dark skinny tie. He looks like a man born to wear a suit. But one button on his white shirt, right above his belt, is undone. And underneath his shirt I can see a small patch of material, a plain white undershirt.

Part of me wants to reach down and poke the professor in as if he were a Pillsbury doughboy come alive. Or button him up. Because I am drawn in, taken by the button undone, by this small evidence of a mistake. At school it's the same: I like best the students who, in their everyday practice of foreign speech, slip and slide and make marvelous mistakes.

Do you like cokie? Kobayashi-kun, a boy at Kasei Junior High asks. By *cokie* he means *cookie*.

Yes, I say, *I eat them all the time.*

Tell me, one girl writes in her notebook, and I smile at the possible ways to reply, *about your brother's thing.*

I try not to stare at the professor's undershirt and I wonder if this is how alluring it is for a man to see a woman's bare ankle from beneath the kimono. A hint of skin. A glimpse of bone. Then the powers-that-be come back into the room and break the spell, announcing that we should all go back to the gymnasium where the winners of the speech contest will be announced.

In the auditorium, I sit next to the professor; Natalie is on his other side. Meanwhile, I look around for Miss Kita and see that she's up in front of the room, talking to Ken'ichi, who looks as though he has survived the ordeal.

Awards are given. Speeches are made. As expected, Miyuki takes home first prize and thanks the judges fluently. My stomach growls and I worry the professor can hear it speak. The body and its embarrassments.

Then it is announced that the speech contest is over and that means the party is, too, and once that's done, once the words have been spoken, we all move to gather in the hallway to put on our coats.

Are you going to the train station? the professor asks.

Natalie and Miss Kita and I all say in unison, *Yes, we are.*

Would you like for me to accompany you?

No, Natalie says. *I can show them the way. We'll be fine.*

Anyway, Miss Kita says, *it was very nice to meet you.*

Anyway, thank you, I add.

Then we all wave like children, which is customary in Japan — *goodbye! goodbye! take care! take care!* — and the professor stands framed in the doorway, unbuttoned and fluent and all alone.

T he next day, I find an excuse to phone Natalie, asking her if she knows of any freelance teaching work. I pretend that I am calling on behalf of a friend. But the talk is a ruse. Finally I get around to asking about what I want.

The professor. Do you know him well?

Oh yes, she says. *Very fluent in English. Very smart too. He's a smart cookie. And he wants to get to know some English-speaking adults. Australians. English. But Americans, especially. He told me he wants to get to know Americans, especially.*

Would I be interested? she asks.

Natalie gives me the professor's phone number and tells me she will also give the professor mine. *You two would probably like each other.* She accomplishes this so effortlessly I think this must be how an *omiai* must work, what a relief it must be to have these small details orchestrated by someone else.

Then, like all good minor characters, Natalie disappears, returning to buttery America where I never hear from her again.

I arrive at our first meeting fifteen minutes late, walking into the professor's office dragging mud from my boots with apologies spilling from my mouth.

I'm sorry, I say. *I had trouble finding your building in the dark. Really, I'm so sorry to be late.*

It's all right, he says, rising. He extends his right hand to shake mine at the same time he bows, just as he did the first time we met.

Dueling gestures, I think. He is a man of two cultures, two ways of relating to the world. And here is when I remember that Natalie gave me this information over the phone. That the professor is married.

That he has a three-year old daughter. That his daughter studies English at the Let's Talk! conversation school.

I am standing in front of the professor, bowing as he says, *I thought perhaps you got lost along the way and that my directions were not as clear as they might have been,* wondering why I have delayed in thinking about this information till now, why it seems so strange to absorb it now, this fact that the professor has two women in his life, a daughter and a wife, a whole complicated *private* private life.

He speaks very formally, clearly, correctly, no missteps at all. Others might say, *I thought Miss Marilyn had some troubles in dark.* But he is smoother than that, this man so buttoned-up and well-spoken tonight.

Yes, I say. *I mean, no. I mean, yes, I got lost but really, your directions were fine. I'm just kind of spacey sometimes. I should have come just a little earlier when it was still light.*

We sit down at a table near his desk and launch into small talk — what the professor will later call *small talks,* only by then, after our relationship has advanced, I won't have the heart to correct him as he has told me I should.

Did you come straight from work?

What kind of courses do you teach?

Do you enjoy the sentō?

Are there certain Japanese foods you especially like to eat?

We speak in small doses, trading the information any two people might. The talk is anonymous, careful, slow. We offer up safe biographies. Where we are from. What we've done. The seduction of facts, I will think later.

Salt Lake City, Utah.

Nagano-ken.

A professor of sociology.

A newspaper reporter. At a small, mediocre paper.

Then the professor asks if I would like some coffee.

Yes, I say. *Coffee would be nice.*

He gets up from his chair and moves toward the small coffee maker, situated on his desk, and I see him once again in relief: a man who, in flipping a switch, demonstrates he has planned very well for this visit, anticipating everything, even coffee, in advance. On the table he has placed a notebook and pencil should confusions arise between us as we converse. The pencil, I see, has a very sharp tip. He has even sharpened his pencil in advance.

Here is a man of patience, I think. Precision. I am moved that his precision involved planning for a visit from me.

He brings me a cup of coffee, asks if I take my coffee black. I lie and say yes, embarrassed at what I perceive to be a fuss.

Then we sip our black coffee quietly, pausing before plunging back into the talk. And after that, it's all talk. We talk for hours upon hours upon hours and keep talking well into the night. We talk about politics, movies, culture, and books. The talk is exhilarating, the talk is a relief. And from this talk, a pattern begins: I ask questions, which the professor answers happily.

Finally, before midnight, still wired on coffee, I say, *This is crazy. I've completely overstayed my welcome, haven't I?*

No, the professor says, *not at all, I have enjoyed every minute of this.*

We both broach the possibility of doing it again.

Would you be interested . . . ?

Perhaps we could . . . ?

We are hesitant, tentative, incredibly shy — innocents still as to what our interest means, conscious only that here it is, this interest, like a newborn child between us, a creature we have no idea how to hold or feed.

We ask each other what we should do.

Meet again?

Yes.

Yes.

He walks me to the elevator, asks will I be OK? *Should I drive you home? I would be happy to.*

Yes, I say. *I mean, no, you don't need to drive me home. I'll be OK.*

Well, OK, then. Thank you for coming, he says.

Thank YOU, I say, buttoning up my Japanese winter coat, a pea coat I bought in Tokyo last year. I wonder how it is that something called *pea* could be such a dark navy blue. I am thinking of something Ken'ichi said the Monday after the ordeal of the speech contest was through. *I am not disappointing to not win. I am very exciting to participate this in.*

Then I'm out into the Nagano night and settled onto the train, thinking about the professor's face, so large and lovely, intelligent and round.

We meet again one evening in the professor's small office and continue talking about a range of topics, about Japanese farms and *samurai* and the ongoing controversy over imported rice. About the Japanese custom of students wearing school uniforms to school. About the Japanese custom of bowing when you meet. We talk about the Japanese custom of engaging in small talk.

The professor says on the surface, small talks look like nothing much at all but in reality small talks allow Japanese people to learn a great deal from one another in a subtle and significant and highly nuanced way.

Then the professor says something unrelated to a public issue.

I have had, he sighs, *a very difficult week.*

What happened? I ask.

Well, really, it's nothing, he says. *But this job — it is not what I had hoped it would be when I was young.*

And this is the night the professor opens up, telling me the sorrows of his professional life, his days as a student activist, how he'd been branded in the sixties because of his Marxist beliefs, so that now he stood no chance of becoming a professor at Tokyo University, his alma mater, the country's most prestigious university, what everyone calls the Harvard of Japan.

And that's what you want? I ask.

He looks surprised, as if he has never thought to question that: what he wants.

It would, he says, *be better than teaching here where the students have no interest in Japanese history, where I cannot make a mark, where I can only get by.*

I tell him about my own thwarted desires, how I want to write but I don't know how. How I keep these notebooks but know the notebooks are not enough. How I don't know what I'm supposed to be doing next. I tell him how all I've ever wanted is to write and to love. How I always wanted a baby too.

We both inch closer and closer toward what we both know is the danger and the thrill: a discussion of our personal lives. And this is the night the professor tells me about his marriage, that he married his current wife — his second — because he knew she would be different, that she would not cheat.

I want to balk, to say, *Oh, really? How can you be sure about that?* But out of respect for the professor I hold my tongue, say nothing, and instead marvel that here we are, talking, and the texture of his consciousness, the fact of his first marriage, and my own desires, so hidden but full — that all of this is beginning to shine through.

We come back to issues, our safe ground, our spot. We talk about *omiai*, arranged marriages, noting pros and cons.

Isn't it interesting, the professor says, *that the meal is such an important part of omiai?*

We mull this over. Think out loud. Decide that two people cannot come together first without the intimacy of sharing a meal, of breaking bread. This is an idea that has never occurred so plainly to me before and it dazzles me, this idea that love is cultivated through bread and water, wine and rice.

The professor pours more coffee and then says he has a question for me but what he asks does not seem like a question at all.

He has been watching American movies, he says. Noticing certain things. That American men and women drink a great deal of coffee in the movies. Have I noticed that? And this as well? That coffee leads to dinner?

These dinners, do they always lead to something else?

I know exactly what the professor wants to know but I never answer directly. Instead, we agree to meet for dinner next time.

The next day, a surprise arrives in the mail: an invitation from Let's Talk! to attend the conversation school's annual English language play Sunday night, three days from now. Natalie must have put me on the school's mailing list before she left Japan. Normally I would throw such an invitation away, but this time I think it might be interesting to show up unannounced, for surely the professor will attend this event too.

Nagano's streets look different on this night and I find myself getting lost, going round and round. By the time I arrive, *Snow White* is underway. I stand uncomfortably in the back of the room, scanning the backs of the audience members' heads, hoping for a glimpse of a man with salt and pepper hair.

But the room is too dark and I cannot see, so I settle in and watch as the play proceeds in its ramshackle way, scene changes taking longer than the play itself, actors stumbling over foreign language lines. And the seven dwarfs, inchoate junior high school boys, marching across the stage solemnly, as if in a funeral procession, looking so melancholy that a few mothers in the back start to giggle out loud and I hear one whisper to another that her son is so serious, so *majime*, she doesn't recognize him!

Then a small movement. A rustle. The professor is beside me, distinguishing himself from the crowd.

I didn't know you'd be here tonight, he whispers, and I whisper back, *It's nice to see you too*, and the play continues and I notice that the huntsman in the play looks like he's in a motorcycle gang, wearing black jeans and a leather jacket and dark glasses, a streak of black-hair-dyed-blond an unholy steeple on his head.

The play stretches, then reaches its pitch.

The prince in his yellow construction paper crown moves toward Snow White to offer a scripted kiss, stepping near her, leaning in. The audience gasps.

What could be more scandalous than this! A kiss!

Then the lights on the stage go out all at once, leaving everyone suspended in the darkness of the room, wondering what will happen next. The pause that by necessity must precede the kiss.

The moment passes. The lights come up, first on stage and then in the auditorium, and the small actors take their bows, introducing themselves one by one.

I am a maid. Thank you.

I am a dwarf. Thank you.

I am a Snow White. Thank you.

I am a Prince. Thank you.

When the applause is through, I turn to the professor and say, *I am a Marilyn. Thank you.*

And he laughs and says, *But what are you DOING here?*

And I say, *I wanted to surprise you.*

And he says, *You definitely did that.*

And he says, *May I introduce you to my wife?*

And it dawns on me that I keep forgetting about this.

The wife. *His* wife. He has a wife. The wife is with him now.

Your wife is here? Where is she? I am smiling, trying to arrange my face as if this is the most natural thing in all the world.

He points to a small, black-haired woman in a plain white shirt and loose black pants. She has short hair. A kind face. She is holding the hand of a three-year-old girl in a small Mickey Mouse parka.

Is that your daughter? I ask.

I am feeling woozy, but not in a familiar watery, fairy-tale way. Now I am feeling woozy and foolish and maybe a little sick. Here is his wife. Here is his daughter. I remember something a junior high school student from Meizen asked me once: *Does Marilyn-sensei know Mickey's lover?* by which she meant Minnie Mouse. I turned red immediately, as if I'd walked in on Mickey and Minnie, teenagers fooling around on some plaid 1970s couch and I told the girl, no, I didn't know Mickey's lover personally.

Yes, the professor says. *Let me introduce you. I've told her all about you.*

The professor's wife is talking to another young mother, another fresh-faced woman holding a little boy's hand. There is a whole club of them here, these lovely young Japanese mothers. Their children study English at the Let's Talk! school.

The children stare at each other. A boy now faces the professor's little girl. I create the story line. Boy meets Girl. Girl meets Boy. Boy points a fat finger at Girl's Mickey Mouse coat. Maybe Boy sees that Girl's zipper's undone.

He has told her all about me.

No, I can't, I say. *I've got to catch the train in just a couple of minutes so I really can't stay. But I did want to see the play and support the school. Weren't those seven dwarfs a hoot?*

A hoot? the professor says.

This is the first time he has not understood a word I have used.

A crack-up, I say. But he still looks perplexed.

Funny, I continue. *You know, they were very funny up there, so sober when they were whistling off key.*

The professor looks uncomfortable as if I have begun speaking in tongues.

Really, I've got to go. But we'll talk soon?

Yes, OK, OK, he says.

And then, I'm gone, running to the train station, lecturing myself along the way, *you stupid girl, you stupid girl,* because now it's clear to me that I've intruded where I had no business intruding at all and anyway, the professor isn't even interested in me. *I've told her all about you,* he said, like he was only interested in the talk all along, like I was just some stupid conversation piece.

In the train, I take a vow of silence.

Well, that's that, then. We will never talk again.

And I berate myself again and again.

I am a stupid. I am a stupid.

A teenage boy with acne gets on at the next stop, spots me and takes the empty seat in front of me. I can guess what will happen next, how he will gather his courage to speak. And he does.

Do you speak English?

Yes, I say.

Will you speak with me today?

I shake my head to answer no. I am cold as winter, hard as nails.

Gomen nasai, I say. *Sorry.*

I want to say to him, *Do you know what these words mean? Cold as winter? Hard as nails? These are idioms. They mean, I am an idiot and language is too.*

But the boy is a boy, no match for cool-hearted me. His face falls in when I tell him no; his face turns red. I want to take my rejection right back, to say to this face now as open as a wound, *I'm sorry, I'm sorry. Of* COURSE *I'll speak some English with you. What would you like to talk about? Disneyland? Mickey Mouse? Do you know Mickey's lover, Minnie, by any chance?*

But I can't take it back. So I sit there, cold as ice, quiet as a tree stump, watching as the boy turns his back to me, leaving me to imagine the downfallen look on his pimply face.

At the next stop, the boy gets off and in his place, a new load of passengers pour in, including a drunken salaryman who moves toward the youngest woman on the train, trying to press his shriveled old raisin of a body against the school girl's soft, ripe one.

She's wearing a knee-length skirt, dark knee socks, a dark brown coat. Her face is stone.

The man lunges, then slurs into her ear, spittle spewing from a ravished face.

The girl, repulsed, turns away.

And if he were young? If he were the handsome boy with the wounded face? The girl slips away into the next car. The car's lights blink on and off, the train tipsy on its feet. The salaryman sinks down into a seat.

I close my eyes and I think how ridiculous the body is with all its unreasonable desires, how ridiculous we all are.

n the days that follow, I go about my business, teaching the Japanese businessmen once a month at night and teaching classes every day at Meizen. A student at Meizen draws pictures during English class. When I confiscate the goods, I find a caricature of Miss Kita and me, a skinny pole next to a wide-eyed blob.

You have some talent, I tell the boy. I return the picture to his desk, take my pencil and draw a frown on the blob with eyes.

The boy hangs his head, says quietly under his breath, *Gomen*.

Later that day at lunch, I am seated next to the principal, who asks me what I think of the Japanese children at his school. I tell him these children need to learn some respect, that they ought to realize even *gaijin* are people too, but I mix up my words in Japanese and wind up telling the principal, *even foreigners are carrots, too*.

After lunch another day, a boy approaches me at my desk in the teachers' room and points and turns bright red.

I assume he's pointing at my breasts wanting to say something about *gaijin* women, how their breasts are so full. Kids here are always talking about that: how the *gaijin* body is so thick, so full, how the *gaijin* nose is so tall, too.

I look him straight in the eye, disgusted. *What?* I ask. These kids are shits, I think, perverted little shits.

Miss Marilyn. The boy stammers. His face is red as the Japanese flag. *Rice, Marilyn-sensei. . . ?*

Yes, I like rice, I say. I have these conversations a dozen times a day. *Do you like rice? Do you like Japan? Do you use chopsticks?*

Then something else comes out.

Miss Marilyn — RICE.

And suddenly I see: I have a glob of dry rice stuck to my shirt.

Gomen nasai, I tell the boy, peeling the golf-ball sized glob off. *Gomen nasai* and *dōmo*. Sorry. Thank you. *Please excuse me.*

Meanwhile, the days tick by.

Meanwhile, the students continue asking, *Does Miss Marilyn like Japan?*

Meanwhile, the phone rings and I ignore it, willing the professor away.

On the last day of February I come home from school to find two letters in my box: an acceptance letter on university letterhead to a graduate program in the United States, a school set in the middle of prairies and cornfields, a school I applied to on a lark. The second is a handwritten note in black ink on a delicate white sheet from the professor. It reads:

Please excuse me my faults.

I want to see you as soon as possible.

In *kanji* and *rōmaji*, as if I might not guess who the note is from, the professor signs his name.

I take both letters inside my apartment, read them each again and again. There is something stirring in the professor's ordinarily eloquent tongue slipping. If his note were perfect, I would not be quite as aroused as I am now.

Please excuse me my faults.

I want to see you as soon as possible.

Taking a hot bath that night and listening to Billie Holiday, I marvel at what a difference a day makes. I have a note from a university saying *yes*, and the university is in *Iowa*, a faraway and dreamy place. I imagine living in a large red barn and keeping chickens and growing tomatoes and reading and writing every day and I also imagine meeting someone. Because who would want to live in that barn all by herself? And then there is the note from someone, from the professor, and the words from his note and the words from the university letter blur, because behind them is the same sentiment, and I just can't get over how good it feels, this perfect February Japanese day, the words behind the words. *You are the chosen one.*

Before falling asleep on a stack of pink futons, I make a decision: I will write back to the people at the school in the prairie to tell them *Yes, I will definitely come.* And I will force myself to wait a week before calling the professor to excuse him his faults. Just one week. A delicious waiting week.

meet the third man during my waiting week. I meet him in the most random of ways: in a CD shop in the Ito-yokado department store where I am on the brink of buying three CDs by Shang Shang Typhoon, an all-girl Okinawan band. It is the kind of impulsive purchase I've been making all week as I wait to call the professor again, as my time in Japan dwindles away, as I both yearn for and dread the coming of spring since spring means summer is coming next and in the summer, I will have to leave, will have to move to dreamy Iowa.

Yesterday it was reams of rice paper, enough to wallpaper a small house; the day before that, three red paper umbrellas, the kind I could buy in the States for a fraction of the price. These trinkets, these CDs — they are an attempt, I know, to weigh myself down, to keep myself from floating away as if I were Dorothy in *The Wizard of Oz,* jumping out of that hot-air balloon to rescue Toto and also trying to rescue herself.

At the CD shop, a man comes up and starts asking questions, the typical ones that *gaijin* ask of one another in every Japanese town.

Where are you from?

How long have you lived in Japan?

What kind of music do you like?

Are you single?

I answer honestly, that I like Japanese reggae pop at the moment, and that yes, I am single, but I'm sighing at the sheer predictability and audacity of this guy. So I start to walk away.

Then Amir asks if I want to have coffee with him and for some reason I can't explain — because he asks so easily, so sincerely, without guile? Because I am, despite a flicker of annoyance followed by a flicker of fear, feeling reckless right now? Because I want to speed along in this waiting week in which I have ordered myself not to call the professor? — I say yes.

Yes. I will have coffee with him. Coffee will be a distraction, a relief.

We will go to a crowded coffee shop downstairs. Sit at a table, surrounded by strangers. Talk about nothing. Nothing, I think, will be very, very nice.

Coffee would be nice.

Amir smiles.

He is tall and dark and looks very, very strong, the physical opposite of the short, stocky, silver-haired professor. A healthy bamboo shoot.

He also looks very, very young, a face full of not-quite-grown-into chiseled features. Not a hint of vanity, it seems. On this afternoon, he's wearing bright white Levi's with a bright neon green parka over a bright orange sweater underneath, which gives him the appearance of a child, since only children in Japan wear colors as bright as this.

He looks like a pimp, my friend Rachel will say one day when winter is done and spring has finally sprung. She will be watching Amir walk away, after the three of us have spent the afternoon hanging out, first in a movie theater, next in a noodle shop, and then in a dark bar where Amir's presence strikes us both as all lightness and relief, so different from the other men we meet, the expatriates from Australia and America who complain so bitterly about all things Japanese.

You mean that as a compliment, right?

Oh, yes, she says. *He's a very handsome man. A very pleasant pimp. Though you might want to get him to tone those colors down just a bit.*

Rachel is an English teacher at a school near mine. She's Australian, used to be a jill-a-roo, and she tells me stories sometimes about her former job, castrating bulls. In those days, she packed a shotgun in the trunk of her car, a fact she says tells you everything about the ranch hands surrounding her at the time.

They'd rape you in a second if given a chance, she says. *Other than that, they were fairly nice guys.*

She takes a purely pragmatic approach to men, asks simply: *Is he a decent fuck? That's the bottom line. Don't let anyone tell you it's not.*

Around his neck Amir wears a thick gold chain that says GOD in capital letters, which on this, our first meeting, I think is too gaudy to bear and I look around as we make our way to the coffee shop, hoping no one I know is here.

Later, I will come to love that chain because the chain will remind me that Amir is my gift from a GOD somewhere, the kind I say I don't believe in anymore, and I will think that maybe GOD, too, is a flashy dresser, someone who might be mistaken for a pimp. A pleasant pimp.

Yes, I say, *this place is fine.*

Then we're sitting and drinking coffee and trading information back and forth. Talking about what we are doing in Japan, what we did before we came. How I had worked as a small-town newspaper reporter, a job I liked but had to leave. How he had been a race car driver but now he didn't own a car.

Neither of us seems impressed or distressed by the information we trade; not overly curious or overly interested or overly anything. We are simply moving effortlessly back and forth in a pleasant exchange. And the talk itself—slow and steady, Amir using the kind of simple Japanese I can understand—clears the cobwebs in my head.

Amir is not at all put off by my pidgin Japanese nor attracted to my frequent lapses into English. Instead, he seems solid, neutral, and safe. I like sitting here, drinking coffee with him, this man who speaks so fondly of his home in Teheran and who speaks so fondly of his housemates in Japan, four Iranian men who, like Amir, work in a noodle factory and who, like Amir, can't go home because they are working illegally in Japan.

What is it you make in that noodle factory? I ask.

Noodles, he says, and there's nothing in his voice that shows he's making fun of me, though now that I've uttered the words, I have to laugh.

Who's buried in Grant's tomb, right?

And when I laugh, so does he.

When we leave the coffee shop Amir takes my hand and asks if I want to have coffee again. Without hesitation, this time I say yes.

Yes.

He doesn't ask for my phone number, which is good since I have irrationally concluded that I won't give him *that* no matter how sweetly he asks.

And for a while, Amir doesn't ask for much. Only that we meet again. Which we do. Always at the same coffee shop underneath a department store called Ito-yokado, which becomes *our* coffee shop, the place we meet before going out for dinner or seeing a movie or walking by the castle in this city, the crow-black castle in the center of town where, perched on top of a seven-story site on my first day in Matsumoto, I scanned the city from small, armor-proof windows, wondering not what life had been like in ancient Japan but what *my* life in this modern country and city would soon be like.

Will I meet him for coffee again?

Yes, I say. The drama is easy, the spectacle smooth. Is this the dream of travel? To so easily move?

Coffee leads to dinner. Dinner to more.

Take care, take care, Amir says each time we part. *People are different everywhere.*

And within two weeks I am entangled in relationships with two men, two more than I am accustomed to, one involving the mind, the other the body. That's how I see the professor and Amir at first: separate from one another, a clean split.

As if such a separations were possible. As if the split wouldn't split.

When I call the professor, he apologizes again and again.

I am very sorry. You must excuse me my faults. You surprised me, that's all. I wasn't sure what to do. Please agree to see me soon.

I don't know, I say.

Just once, he says.

I don't think so. I don't think it's a good idea.

The professor pushes and his pushing interests me. Like a dish of raw horse meat at a party — sheer novelty.

All relationships come out of some misunderstanding, he says.

But you seemed indifferent to me at that play the other day. And anyway, I'm leaving the country soon. Did you know?

No.

A pocket of silence. A lull. These are the moments where two people sink or swim.

As for indifferent, he says, *I am not.*

We decide to swim. I agree to dinner. I invite the professor to my house.

It will be very simple, I say. *I'm not knocking myself out.*

Knocking?

I'm not going to any trouble, I say. *For you. For anyone.*

And our conversation ends with me instructing him to bring two bottles of wine. *An American custom,* I say.

The professor draws a leaf of spinach from the plate and holds it up to the candlelight.

What is it? he asks.

I smile. I have expected this. What is ordinary in America becomes exotic here.

Raw spinach, I say. *Sometimes Americans like to eat their spinach raw instead of cooked.*

We are in my kitchen, sitting at a small crowded table. The professor eats a single leaf and says, *Yes, I see why. This is very good. But we Japanese do not know about this.*

He finishes the vegetable soup I have prepared; I finish off the first bottle of wine. Then we sit back and watch the candles shrink and the night open up and the professor asks why I came to Japan.

I want to tell him about how my life used to be, not its facts exactly but its temperature, how the temperature went up and down in the United States, how I used to drive all over a desert state listening to songs by Patsy Cline and Patty Loveless and Willie Nelson and Darden Smith, and how every state seemed like a state of longing to me. I want to tell him how I liked my job writing newspaper stories at that time, liked it because it gave me something marginally purposeful to do, but I also hated it because I knew I was only reporting on other people's lives because I didn't know how to inhabit my own.

I want to tell him how, when I left for Japan, I told my American co-workers, *I'm leaving the country, I'm making a clean split,* and those who were married with children sighed and shook their heads and said how lucky I was to be leaving just like that, lickety-split, and I knew what they meant and I'd smile and say, *yes, I'm so lucky to go to live in Japan,* and part of me felt lucky, it really did, but there was this other part, the part I'd leave out, another way of describing all that freedom I felt: that I was crushed by what others considered good luck, paralyzed by the dizzying choices ahead. That I wasn't going for any high-minded reason — to learn a new language, to study the culture, to experience adventure — or any reason, really, at all, except that time-honored reason so often behind travel: that desperate desire to escape my own solitary, unsatisfying, singular skin.

I want to tell the professor all of this, that all I ever wanted was a guy and a garden and some babies and some books. That I didn't understand how it happened, this ending up alone over and over again. I want to tell him about the man I used to love, how I went to see him one night after signing the contract to teach in Japan.

We made dinner in his small kitchen that night, and spoke easily as we always had. We finished our meal and washed the dishes and left them to dry on a rack. And after that, I found myself telling this man what I knew about this job in Japan: how the money promised to be very good, almost double what I was making now; how it meant traveling to three different junior highs; how I would have to leave soon, in just one more month; and then something I had not planned to say.

If you say 'stay,' I will.

He put the dishtowel down and waited as if he imagined I might have something else to add and then said as gently as anyone ever has, *Go.*

How do I tell the professor that? That I craved then as I still crave now all the complications and burdens of ordinary love?

I'm not sure, I say. *I guess I was unhappy. That's all.*

The professor nods sympathetically. He knows something of unhappiness. I get up to put the kettle on the burner and suggest we move to the living room, beyond the glass doors to a place where dried roses hang from the walls and futons are spread on the floor.

This is for me a very strange thing, he says.

The professor stares at the futons, which now seem embarrassing out there for all the world to see. It is as if I have told him a dirty joke, or lifted my skirt during dinner to show him sexy underwear, the kind I don't wear.

It just seems like a lot of work to roll them up every day. I mean, I live alone. I figured it would be all right.

There is something very— the professor stops.

I wait for him to find the word.

Provocative, he says. *There is something provocative in this.*

I should be more embarrassed than I am and for a moment that's exactly what I pretend to be: innocent of the rules here, embarrassed to have crossed some invisible line. My hand flies to my face; I say, *Gomen nasai.*

But we both know we are flirting now around the edges of this, a mock misunderstanding. We both know there is something else we want now, something we crave.

He sits down on a cushion positioned at the edge of the futon.

I go to the kitchen as the kettle whistles and return with two small blue cups and a pot of hot *soba* tea on a tray.

I can guess what will happen next.

How we will continue talking as the tea gets cold. How he will take my hand in his, never looking me in the eye. How he will touch my hair. How I will say, *We shouldn't.* How the body lies.

Why then am I troubled when he asks in model sentences, so perfect, so polite —

May I kiss you?

May I unbutton your blouse?

Yes, I answer.

May I fall in love?

And then, to that last one, no.

Absolutely not.

Now I am wide awake, the sequence of actions — first touch, first kiss, first question invoking love — conspiring to make me sit up straight quite literally.

Look, you're married, I say, buttoning my shirt. *We shouldn't be doing this.*

And this becomes my excuse, my stated reason for backing out of consummating the affair: that he is married, which it's true, matters a great deal to me, has long been something I did not see as a possibility. *Do not lie, do not litter, do not cheat with someone's other.* My moral foundation in a sing-song rhyme.

But what I'm really thinking in the heat of the moment is more embarrassing than that. What I'm really thinking is that the professor's kiss was too *needy* for me, and that maybe the sex to follow won't be good enough for all the trouble this affair will be.

The fucking tonight would have to be fucking great to make up for the hassles of getting involved with him.

This is what I am thinking, a thought that all these years later gives me a chill.

The professor looks confused.

Yes, it's true, I am, he says. *I am a married man. But you have always known this.*

Look, I say, staring at his socks, a small pattern of triangles, black on navy blue, *it's true. I have always known this. You are married. But right now I feel like I'm understanding what that means.*

What does that mean? he asks.

He reminds me of a boy at Shinmei Junior High, a boy so moon-faced and earnest he breaks my heart. The boy's always leaving me notes that don't have any messages except FROM SHINODA written in letters, each one a different colored pen. I receive each note, wondering if there's something else, some message written in invisible ink. But there's never anything more, there's never anything at all past his name.

It means that this would be — that this is — well, it's wrong. I mean, I don't know what either of us can say beyond that, you know?

I am trying to remember how men have always rejected me, the words they must have chosen so carefully to preserve some dignity. I remember the men who came before, the ones who stayed a week, sometimes a month, once in a while a year or more, the ones who brought presents — a clove of garlic for when I was sick; a pot of dirt from which basil grew — and wonder now why I didn't appreciate them more, these men who were fond of me but not in love, these men who found a way to tell me with some measure of kindness, *I'm sorry but . . .*

But nothing. None of their words come back.

Maybe if you weren't married, I say. *If circumstances were different . . . If you didn't have a child . . .*

The professor nods. Looks relieved. At least I am willing to discuss this with him.

All of this is true, he says. *But it's not what's important.*

Maybe not to you. But you have to respect my position here.

Meanwhile, my mind reels with what seems true: that lying is a way of protecting myself; that I am less worried about actually *being* a shit than being found *out* by the professor as being a shit. I do not want to deal with the professor's pain on top of my own guilt right now.

Instead of looking disappointed, the professor looks exhilarated, as if he has not heard rejection in anything I have said, as if we have just begun the important part of our relationship instead, the part that will take on these issues of talking about us.

You should go, I say.

Yes, OK, OK. But we have not finished this.

Then he stands as I stand, and I fold my arms over my chest and he does the same, and I cringe at the Simon Says quality of this, and I begin to usher him toward the door and he lingers in the *genkan*, taking his time as he puts on his coat and slides into shoes and I stare at them, I can't help myself. His shoes. The shoes of a middle-aged man. *You are still young,* I tell myself. *You are not so desperate as to need this man.*

I will see you soon, the professor says.

He is confident, oblivious. I have fixed him dinner, he has touched my skin. This is all that registers on that open face.

I enjoyed dinner very much. You are a very good cook.

I laugh and say, *Well, that's a first. No one's ever told me that.* But the flirtation, I know, has run its course. The joke is no joke. I keep my arms folded, my fingers out of unruly hair. Instead, I pat the strand of silver hair sticking up out of the professor's head and feel a burst of tenderness blossom all over again.

Good night, he says, but still he lingers, still he refuses to move.

Good night, I say, feeling powerful and guilty and tired and confused. Frustration turns to tenderness, tenderness to this: irritation of my own making. I have made my futon and now refused to sleep in it, so to speak. So there's this, too, I think: a price to pay not for having an affair but for backing out of one, too.

I move past the professor, open the door and step outside the apartment in my bare feet, a blast of cold air smacking my skin. I pretend to find out what the weather is, to look up at the nighttime sky.

The gesture works. The small talk has its desired effect. The professor follows and finally waves goodbye and I fly back inside, eager to curl up in sleep.

The dream of travel, of living overseas, is the dream of having it both ways. To have your home and to leave it too, to eat your cake and your sushi too, to be involved and also to stand at a remove, to be a *part* of something — to find ways to fit — and to stand apart, experiencing a country's foreignness.

At times the paradox doesn't seem paradoxical at all. At times you're just going along happily in this foreign place and the country seems different but not so different from what you knew before so that even the squid on the pizza seems just right and the rules of etiquette are challenging but not oppressively so. You remember that you don't leave chopsticks standing up straight in a bowl of rice because it's a sign of death; you do not wear bathroom slippers anywhere but in the bathroom stall because to do so is — well, it's just gross, that's all.

You go along and you adapt and you change and you are young, you are still so young, and you are so lucky to be living in a foreign country and you find yourself wondering why the whole world doesn't have squatter toilets because they make more sense, really, your butt never touching the porcelain, and you're fine, you're very nearly fitting in, and you have these friends, these women who meet you for coffee and who tell you their secrets over slender pieces of chocolate cake and then you tell them your secrets too, and you leave each café saying, *Ureshii, I'm happy,* and knowing for once what *happy* means. And you *are* happy. You have a life. A job. An apartment. Interesting women friends. You meet these friends for coffee and spill your secrets over silken chocolate pie. And you have errands to run. Always, errands. And there is routine in these errands. Every Saturday you buy these tulips from a certain old woman because no one could be unhappy bringing tulips home to put in a blue and white vase on the kitchen table.

And the things that happen that should bother you never bother you, like the children who, as you're pedaling by, shout out *Gaijin, Kowai!* which at first you think means *Oh, what a cute foreigner there!* but soon you find out it means *What a scary-looking alien!* And still, you don't care. You're pedaling by on a bike with a basket, your skirt billowing wildly in the wind, and you have the urge to cackle sometimes as if you were the Wicked Witch of the West. And all you can think is *Oh, what a world, what a world* when the drunken salarymen shout out, *How much?* as if you were a prostitute, as if you would ever sleep with them.

And then something happens and usually it's small — the Japanese businessmen whisper something about the woman with radish-shaped legs and you're sure this time, they're talking about you — or you bite into a croissant filled with mayonnaise, a croissant you thought was perfectly plain — and you hate it here, you hate the mayonnaise, you hate the men, you think with a force of clarity that catches you off guard, *I hate it here* and *I don't belong.*

And then you're back for a visit in your home country, back in the United States and something happens *there* — you're in an airport and you're walking toward a vending machine and your ten-year-old nephew's beside you, chatting away, and just as you pull out two cans of Coke, he says, *Watch out for razor blades,* and you say, *What?* and he says, *Watch out for razor blades. Didn't you know? Somebody's been putting razor blades into Coke cans lately. Didn't you know?* and you say, *No, I didn't know* and you wonder how it is possible that this boy, only ten years old, how can he know about razor blades in Coke cans? and you also think *I can't wait to get out of here,* can't wait to get back to that *other* place, that *other* home, that *other* country, which, days earlier, you couldn't wait to leave, only this time you want to take your ten-year-old boy with you, too, just steal him from his mother, your sister, because he is way too young for this crazy shit, because this is a boy too precious for razor blades and just the other day, you took him to an amusement park and he sang to you on the ferris wheel and he squealed in the bumper cars and at lunch time, after eating his burger, he went up to the girl at the concession stand to ask for a *curtsy water* instead of courtesy water and you are going to take him back to Japan with you now, just slip him in your pocket and take him back.

And then you're back, back in Japan, the country that doesn't seem like the *other* one anymore, the one that used to seem foreign but now seems like home, a *better* home maybe because at least here, there aren't razor blades in Coke for crying out loud, and anyway, you're home again, back in the land of black-haired children and soft-spoken women and sleepy-eyed men and back to riding trains so quiet they're almost like church, and you're going along, riding the train or catching a bus or flying along again on your trusty, rusty Japanese bike, skirt billowing again, hair flying again, children squealing again, and you're in it, this life, you're very much in the thick of it, the center of it, and you're loving your bike, the big basket on your bike, and you're eating your *ramen* and practicing your verbs and you're minding your own business and loving every day, loving the particulars of every day in this country, the one that seems like your own for now, and it's all so wonderful, the *ramen*, the *sentō*, the children, and the gorgeous wash of *pachinko* lights at night, and then again something happens.

Something innocuous. Something small.

You're standing on a street corner, waiting for the light. You're in a crowd of people and everyone's waiting for the light. There are no cars in the intersection. The light remains red. Something rises in you. An urge to move, to cross against the light. And you wonder, doesn't anyone else feel this urge too? A desire to break this one tiny rule? To *move*?

For a split second you're stuck, hovering over the scene as if watching from the outside and for a moment, you glimpse the whole ridiculous comedy of it all, the whole of humanity waiting for this goddamned light, all the throngs of people who have ever lived, and this is what they spend their time doing? Waiting for a traffic light? And it's funny but it's also just about the loneliest you have ever been, and then, the light changes and the world shifts and you're in a new groove, out of that glimpse you had back there of infinity or what-ever that was, back into the ordinary and lovely and everyday flow, and you're walking across the street with your bike, going slow, then you're on the bike, riding downhill past rice fields fast, fast, fast, and you're back into the comfort of a normal routine and you wonder, is this how it goes?

Is this the conundrum travel always presents? That *here* becomes *there*? That *us* becomes *them*? That in a split second the ledger will hide, then reveal itself, and the split will split, then make itself whole? That the whole loop will loop back on itself again and again and again and again?

When Rachel and I meet for coffee I tell her nothing of the professor or my lingering crush on Nozaki of the Japanese businessmen. I tell her only of Amir. How Amir's a good kisser. And more than that. How competent he is at everything.

He cut my hair the other day, I say. *Have I told you this? That he used to be a hair stylist in Tokyo?*

Amir's good for you, Rachel says.

By which she means Amir might loosen me up.

Do you think you might be — god, I hate to even use the word — in love?

Maybe, I say. I'm just testing the idea out. *But I doubt it.*

I do. Our time together is passionate but its temperature — or its type, perhaps — is not enough. No, not *not* enough. But not quite right.

I think maybe we won't cause the other trouble enough.

Rachel nods. Understands. Agrees. *Trouble is everything.*

She is of the opinion that sex and love can't be bedfellows, anyway, so this particular split seems fine to her. The ideal situation: a decent bloke, an above-average fuck.

She knows, too, that woman does not live on fantasy alone, that it's not enough to lust after the boys at school, which we do.

The boys, the boys — are the boys the blueprint to all this desire in Japan?

Is it all the boys here or just a few? I asked Rachel once.

All of them, she said. *No, just a few. I don't know. A few are dangerous.*

Dangerous, how? I ask.

You know . . . dangerous because you know they know you like them and who knows what could happen then.

The boys are ten years younger than Rachel, fifteen years behind me. She is old enough to be their sister. I am closer to a mother's age. We speculate, wondering out loud about the attraction we feel and what it means. We know it's because we're alone here and often lonely. And because we're in a foreign country, everything, including the mundane, takes on an erotic gloss.

Sometimes I think it's maternal, this feeling I have for the boys at school, this desire to protect them, this urge to claim them as my own. Sometimes I think it's more complicated than that, a desire I know but can't name.

Only a few I can identify by name. Most I know only by physical detail.

The boy with a limp who loves Picasso.

The boy who carries my books to class, unasked.

The boy who slouches during English class and doodles in a notebook, but watches me to see if I'm watching him, which I am. All the time. He plays basketball and I watch him play, his thighs so muscular, so familiar, I could pick them out in a lineup of legs in two seconds flat.

There's the boy with a pock-marked face who yawned once in class at the same moment I did. We've exchanged looks in the hallways ever since, conspiratorial half-smiles, then we both get embarrassed and look away.

There's the boy who hands me something after lunch, *Presento*, he says, then races off, waving and shouting out good-naturedly, *Have a NICE day!*, a phrase made popular on Japanese TV. I thank him twice, once in English and again in Japanese. Then I look at what he has handed me: two packets of mayonnaise.

There are the boys in seventh grade, some so small that they float in bunched-up paper bag pants, the boys that make you put your hand to your grown-up teacherly heart. These are the boys who hold hands walking down the hall, who sit in each other's laps, and after a time, you don't see anything strange about all that touching at all. By eighth grade, the acne begins and so does the acting out and you wonder how anyone survives eighth grade anywhere. By ninth grade they begin to divide themselves up, forming cliques and camps that will continue the rest of their lives.

In one group, the good boys, sweet as sunflowers, soothing as *soba* tea—the boys who do their homework every night, study hard in class, and run for student council and go on to universities. In the other camp, boys who cut classes, wear striped socks, and turn their hair orange or red with dye. These are the boys who play poker in the back of class, who smoke outside, who climb onto the roof of the school, walking around in packs.

Just like animals, the Japanese teachers say, worried and ashamed.

These are the boys you run into sometimes late at night, when you're riding your bike home from this or that bar. They're squatting in dark alleys, smoking cigarettes. And sometimes the boys, the good and the bad, visit you at home, fixing your *shōji* doors once in an afternoon of surprise repairs or stopping by to try to build a house of cards while you fix a feast of Coke and French toast.

The house of cards falls flat that day but the afternoon is fine—a few hours spent with boys whose faces are soft as their soft flannel shirts. One boy writes a note afterward in elegant script: *Thank you. I am much obliged* and you will wish you had a way to say, no, *I'm* the one who is beholden to you. For you are a woman alone. These boys' presence is a private present for you.

At school they write messages on the bottom of composition books, little lost boats you have the urge to keep and save. KEEP ON JAMMIN all in caps. Or questions that sail in on paper scraps, tiny letters in bottles that sail across the sea. *Do Marilyn-sensei like Guns and Roses?*

A little, you lie. You believe in kindness over honesty.

They learn from repetition, from writing sentences again and again, and you do, too, only the lesson you learn is that repetition can be ritual, that there's comfort in routine. And this talk, however simple, keeps you afloat.

There are the boys at school whose indifference acts as a veneer and the boys who act eager, but in both cases it's clear: all of them have wants and needs as large and secret and evident as yours. They want science class to end soon and the principal to cut his speeches short. They want to do well at basketball. Get into the drama club. Talk to a girl at lunchtime. Horse around instead of submit to tasks, to study or to clean. They want to read comic books during class. Pass the high school entrance exam. Go to college, marry, have children, and go to work. They want to visit Brazil and China, Australia, and Spain. Become sushi chefs. Basketball players. Construction workers. Engineers. Become lawyers and professors and noodle makers.

What's the most important thing? you ask during English class. *School. Cars. Food. Sleep. Peeing when you have to pee. I want freedom,* another answers. *I want to wear clothes. . . no uniform. I want to go to 7-Eleven on way to school.*

Sometimes, it's true, it is the bad boys you like the best, the ones who are smart and smart-alecky, eager and wild. One boy dyes his black hair brown, wears his bangs long and scraggly instead of neatly cut short. He wears striped socks with his uniform. And he cuts all his classes but then hangs out in the teachers' room.

Once, after you finished correcting a stack of notebooks, he pulled up a chair next to your desk and tried to find a way to talk. His English wasn't very good, your Japanese was even worse. So you looked at the pictures in some magazines you'd brought, and you asked the simplest questions you could.

Who is the prettiest? you asked, pointing at advertisements for cars and movies and beautiful models, airbrushed and thin. *Which ones do you like best?*

He answered each question as best he could, but stopped you on the last one, and reminding you that desire isn't about categories or numbers, that desire isn't about anything solid at all, said in an unmistakably serious tone, *Marilyn-sensei, "pretty" isn't a one-two-three thing.*

After coffee, out on the street, Rachel and I pass a group of boys in school uniforms. One steps forward, offers his hand as if he's some knight we've been waiting for.

Good evening, ladies, he says, in a voice too deep for his teenage years.

We laugh out loud. The boy's buddy corrects him. *Good AFTER-NOON.*

Rachel loves the energy of these boys, their spontaneity, their charm, and I'm taken in by how silly they tend to be. On the streets here, men are serious, sober, it seems, even when they're drunk. Work comes first, not playing around. With the boys, it's different. We act as witnesses to their last chance of letting loose. And maybe we hope to protect them somehow, save them from the future that we know will come. We wonder too what would happen if someone made a move.

Do you ever think. . . ? I ask, as Rachel and I continue down the street, the boyish knight and his cronies behind us now.

It's impossible to imagine, Rachel says. *They carry Sesame Street pencil cases. They turn red when we look them straight in the eye.*

We should read Lolita *again,* I say. *Maybe this time, we'll relate.*

And with that, all talk of men and the boys ends and we turn our attention to the one thing that matters more than anything else: food.

At a small fruit shop, the plums, we agree, look especially fine. But neither of us can remember the verb *to wash,* so we mime to the shopkeeper, *Will you wash these plums, please, for us?*

We dance and we giggle, feeling no embarrassment or shame. Words fail us here, they always have and always will. Desire, like travel, is a spectacle that shines.

The man at the fruit shop laughs, then disappears, emerging from behind a blue curtained door, carrying six plums for us, ripe and dripping wet.

O ne night I meet the professor at a coffee shop that I think of as the Adultery Coffee Shop, since a woman I know has conducted—is this the word? *conducted?* it makes me see her as someone standing in front of violinists, naked, baton in hand—an affair with a certain married man. The two used this coffee shop as their secret place to meet.

The coffee shop is light and airy and full of lots of tables made of blond polished wood and along the walls are shelves where the owners have artistically arranged various blue and white bowls and plates and cups and it strikes me as strange that this is the place where clandestine affairs take place and I wonder if people have, at various times, in the midst of a fight, wanted to smash those beautiful blue and white dishes to the ground.

The professor buys us two cups of coffee, the coffee, we know, a poor substitute for the breaking of bread. Then we plunge into talk, the talk that will replace whatever else we might have done. The talk is a coil, a snake, a rope. We circle round and round too many words we know and when fluency traps us, we begin to choke.

I just don't want you to hate me when I go.

Why would I hate you? he asks.

I don't know.

But I do. I know. Lust has been replaced now by guilt. I am consumed by what the professor will think, as if I were running for office.

I just think we have to stop doing this.

What is this?

This talking around and around all the issues we have.

And what might these issues be?

What we want. What we are . . . to each other—what we are—what we want to be—

The professor has nothing to say to this.

Because there are no labels to help us, no words to save us. Because we are, I think, not a sinking ship but a small, unfit and failing little canoe, one that never managed to leave its own barren shore.

And now this moment of silence fills the air, fills our untidy boat with the water we fear. I am relieved to be quiet, relieved that for one small second we are not rushing in to fill the space between us with words.

I make a wish: Let it die today, this affair that will never be.

Let's talk about something else, he says.

The moment of silence ends. The words decide for us, the words say we will continue to pretend.

OK, I say. *How about your wife.*

The professor flinches.

I have a desire to remind myself she is real, to offer up particulars of who she is. Because right now, the monotony of sex seems a better choice than the monotony of talk. Because right now the sex remains a possibility if only as a strategy to shut us up.

What does she look like? I ask. *What do you talk about at night? Does she cook breakfast in the morning or is that your job?*

If I know the particulars of her, if she's not abstract—

He answers each of my questions as if scoring points for a serious test.

She is ordinary housewife—thin, short-haired, quiet, demure. *We talk about our daughter.* Ordinarily, he fixes breakfast, not her. *She very much enjoys to sleeping late.*

I smile at this. The reality of this. A woman enjoying to sleeping late. I think about the professor's daughter, what kind of girl, then woman, she'll become. If she'll want to travel, for instance. If she'll fall in love with a married man.

So I'm not the typical Japanese husband, he concludes, a finishing remark that leaves me angry, seeing red, for what I hear in these words is an attempt to impress me, not speak openly or honestly of his marriage or wife.

I stare into an empty coffee cup, still as a stone.

Maybe I should take you home, he says.

Yes, I agree.

We drive in silence. I watch out the window as the blue-tiled houses flash by in the early evening light, and I dream of the future, of Iowa, where I fantasize there are houses with large open porches and no professors and lots of trees.

One afternoon at Royal Host, a Denny's-style restaurant — sunny like the Adultery Coffee Shop but filled with more plastic than wood — we try to avoid the subject that continues to dominate us, which is us.

We try discussing politics, hoping to return to the safety of our intellectual *omiai*.

But when the professor begins to lecture, I feel myself falling asleep, as if I were reading a book in tiny nine-point type.

I stay alert long enough to hear what the professor says he wants to make clear: that he believes in the necessity of the importation of foreign rice, that he longs for a restructuring of the Japanese university system, and that the importance of marriage as a social institution cannot, will not, be denied.

I hope, he says, *that you will marry someday.*

I stare into my coffee cup.

And why is that? I ask, refusing to look up.

For the security of it, the comfort of it. I hope you have the experience when you return to the United States.

I ignore the irony, bite hard on my tongue. I remember a Japanese woman I met only a few weeks ago, who said: *And when you return to America you will find a husband?* as if such a thing were like choosing a cantaloupe.

Still I can't imagine it, can't imagine walking down an aisle in a frilly white dress as big as a cake, participating in a ceremony where afterward guests would throw rice. I remember what the Japanese woman said when she first heard of the custom of throwing rice at a wedding in the United States. *Why rice?* asked the woman who wanted me to find my one true cantaloupe. *Why not bread?*

And I smile now at the thought of a wedding where guests afterward throw big chunks of bread, white bread and wheat bread and deep dark brown pumpernickel bread, even frosted-covered raisin bread, bread peppered with nuts, all that bread raining down on a woman in white, a woman I cannot, hard as I try, even at the most absurd of ceremonies, imagine as me.

T he professor tells me he has something important he wants to ask.

May I visit you one day in America?

And before I can answer, he shows me how, on a small white piece of paper he has been carrying in his wallet for who knows how long, he has calculated how much money he would save in a year if he quit taking English lessons at the Let's Talk! school.

He can use that money to visit me in the States, he says.

I hold the tiny slip of paper with numbers on it and am moved that this man has done the math on us, figured a way to concoct a future even while our present, at best, remains precarious.

You'd be welcome, I tell him, and I'm pleased with myself for this tone of politeness I affect, *to visit me in the United States anytime, you know. And of course I would love to meet you for dinner, for instance, if you happened to fly through some city near where I happen to live. But please don't come on my account,* I say.

Why? he asks.

Just don't, I say.

The professor stares out the window, then says it's selfish of me to deny him his dream.

Even, I ask, *if the dream involves me?*

One night in class with the Japanese businessmen, I write the words GUILT and SHAME in big block letters on the blackboard of our messy little classroom in an attempt — a feeble one, I admit in retrospect — to raise the level of discourse for once. Maybe I'm just tired of hearing all the talk about sex. Or maybe I'm trying to impress someone who sometimes shows up and sometimes doesn't.

Tonight he has shown up, Nozaki has, and I am trying to explain what the anthropologist Ruth Benedict said in her book *The Chrysanthemum and the Sword* about the distinction between shame-based cultures and guilt-based cultures so I can ask the businessmen what they think.

Benedict writes:

A society that inculcates absolute standards of morality and relies on men's developing a conscience is a guilt culture by definition, but a man in such a society may, as in the United States, suffer in addition from shame when he accuses himself of gaucheries which are in no way sins. He may be exceedingly chagrined about not dressing appropriately for the occasion or about a slip of the tongue. In a culture where shame is a major sanction, people are chagrined about acts which we expect people to feel guilty about. This chagrin can be very intense and it cannot be relieved, as guilt can be, by confession and atonement. A man who has sinned can get relief by unburdening himself. This device of confession is used in our secular therapy and by many religious groups which have otherwise little in common. We know it brings relief. Where shame is a major sanction, a man does not experience relief when he makes his fault public even to his confessor. So long as his bad behavior does not "get out into the world" he need not be troubled and confession appears to him merely a way of courting trouble. Shame cultures therefore do not provide for confessions, even to the gods. They have ceremonies for good luck rather than for expiation.

I don't quote Benedict verbatim. I don't use words like *expiation* or *chagrin*. What I do is try to boil down the concept by writing two lists on the blackboard, one with *America* and *guilt* and *Judeo-Christian* and *private sin* on it, the other with *Japan* and *shame* and *Buddhism* and *Shinto-ism* and *public honor*. All this in an effort to pose questions: *About what do you feel shame? About what do you feel guilt? And what do you think about the distinction between the two?*

The Japanese businessmen struggle to understand. They are trying, they are, bless their hearts, and a wave of tenderness comes over me as I see them attempt to make sense of these complicated words on the blackboard and I am wondering now if I have summarized Benedict right and I am also wondering why I'm so interested in the distinction myself, which now seems too subtle to worry much about, and I'm also feeling guilty because look at all the trouble I have caused. Or is it shame I am feeling right now?

The businessmen consult with one another, the higher-level students translating from English to Japanese for the beginners. Everyone consults their dictionaries, looking up "private" and "sin" and "public" and "honor" and instead of feeling proud of the fact that there's some serious language work that's getting done instead of the free-for-all of jokes that's usual here, I begin to redden in embarrassment. Because they try and try, but finally it's clear; it's no use. The lesson is a flop.

Miss Marilyn, Mr. Kata said. *We rather — sex — talk!*

And I see that this lesson was a bad idea, that its substance has escaped us all.

All but one. One remains attentive. One nods his head again and again. He is more talkative on this night than ever before. He likes the philosophical nature of this lesson, likes the attempt to talk about something profound. He smiles frequently. Says yes, this is true. Guilt or shame. This is the difference between America and Japan. This is the crux: the difference between inward sin and outward failure. He takes the discussion further. Suggests that the paradigm, though useful, isn't set.

He doesn't use those words, of course. *Crux. Inward. Paradigm. Set.* Maybe he doesn't even talk that much. But in my memory here's how it happens. He's talking and I'm talking and he's listening and I'm listening and in some miracle of miracles it's all complicated and exhilarating and it's also making miraculous sense.

For example? I ask.

For example, he says, he may be Japanese, meaning he is from a culture of shame, but perhaps he is more American deep in his heart.

For example, he says, he sometimes feels the pangs of guilt.

For example?

He doesn't answer directly, but continues talking, saying he thinks the country to which one is born is not necessarily the country of the soul. I am no longer listening to anything other than him and also the ticker tape in my head, evaluating, judging. Discrimination as a form of love.

He isn't like the other Japanese businessmen. He isn't like the professor or Amir. He is intense and detached; involved and indifferent; a man who feels guilt in a country of shame.

In a few weeks he moves to the center of my story, becomes the reason I feel such an unruly mix of guilt and chagrin and exhilaration and shame. In a few weeks, he becomes the reason a new definition of travel emerges for me. Travel as seduction. Travel as education. Travel as a way to move to *be* moved. I will get wrapped up in him, then come wildly undone.

And during this time when I am crazy happy and then crazy in love and then just crazy crazy, I only vaguely understand what will seem so obvious later on: This is why a woman travels halfway across the world. For a time in its chaos that's more real than anytime before. For a time that becomes holy, thinking about it afterward.

Te Japanese businessmen throw me a farewell party, one that follows standard form. There's something comforting in this, in going to parties where you know ahead of time what the party will be: a formal sit-down dinner to start, then informal drinking at a karaoke bar, then a third party, a whiskey-drenched soirée into the early hours of morning, at a local hostess bar.

Nozaki arrives to Party #1 late. No surprise there. But when I look up and see him coming in through those perfectly split curtains, a staple of every restaurant's entranceway here, the sight of him ushers in a specific thrill.

He bows, I nod.

For Miss Marilyn, a private gift, he says. I've already received two gifts from the businessmen: a single elegant lacquer teacup with a delicate lacquer saucer and spoon (which I imagine they have purchased for me because I am a woman alone and they envision me drinking tea in a solitary state) and a nylon travel bag (which they have reason to expect I will use very soon). I have told the businessmen that I will be traveling in Asia on the heels of leaving Japan and I have enjoyed saying just that, that *I will be traveling in Asia and traveling alone,* just as two years ago I enjoyed telling people, *I'm leaving the country, I'm making a clean split,* and the businessmen have responded by asking, *Is Marilyn-sensei nervous about doing such a thing?* and I have returned their concern with false bravado, saying, *Yes, of course, it's an excellent thing,* that *many gaijin women like to travel alone,* that *it is very much an American custom.* I have loved making these pronouncements without worrying if they're true.

Truth is, I do not *want* to go. I have no desire to go to Thailand once again, no desire to see Indonesia, to drop in on Vietnam. I have no compulsion to go trekking or sightseeing, to push my body toward adventure or flight. What I want is to stay here a few more months, to linger longer in a country that I wish were mine. What I want is not to muddy my memories of one place with a host of new ones from another. And then there are the men. The professor. Amir. Why leave when things are still so up in the air? My business feels unfinished here.

Some scheming results in an alternate plan: I'll move out of my apartment and finish up in my three junior highs, but then go to work at my friend, Natsume-san's ABC School, located above her husband's liquor shop, and stay in Natsume-san's extra room. Foreigners are staying there all the time. Her family, she says, won't notice, won't mind. Or I can stay with another teacher from the ABC School, depending on which town — Matsumoto or Shiojiri — I want to wake up in. I can work this out. And I can, I think, justify this all quite easily. Argue that the decision is one of practicality. For I can save more money by working in Japan a few more months. Save more money by giving up the Asian travel. And maybe, I think, save something of myself.

Nozaki's gift comes unwrapped — something I've seen only once during my stay in Japan — and that he has given me this gift in front of the other businessmen surprises me, as I imagine perhaps it surprises them.

It is a small book, no bigger than my hand: the poetry of Shōji Ozawa, his favorite writer, Nozaki explains, as I stand before him, accepting the gift, the book, the gesture with two hands, not one, as is custom here.

Please read, he says.

I will, I say.

Later, my friend Chieko will translate some of the poems for me, which she accomplishes with difficulty, since, as she says, in translation so much nuance naturally gets lost.

That night, though, nothing is lost. Not on us. Not on me. Not on Nozaki. The night is wrapped in *fukusa,* a perfect square of silk.

Thank you, I tell him, blushing fiercely, smiling wide, holding onto that book and wondering about those beautiful squiggles inside.

We sit down at the long table where dinner is served. Nozaki, following etiquette, sits on the opposite end of the table from me so

that the senior members of the businessmen can sit in the supposedly privileged spot, next to the teacher. Such a shame, I think, since
Mr. Yoshida and Mr. Kato are only going through the motions, asking
me questions to be polite. They are as tired of me as I am of them.

Then we're off to the second party, singing karaoke at a typically
smoky bar. "Yesterday" and "My Way." I am embarrassed for Nozaki
to hear me sing off-key. Also, I have worn a tweed jacket over a light-
knit sweater and skirt and I'm boiling hot but I don't dare take my
jacket off for fear Nozaki will think I look fat.

So I'm getting hotter and hotter as the night goes on and the beer
is flowing and the whiskey is flowing and Nozaki is sitting beside
me — at the second party, the formal etiquette goes — and then, in
what seems a small but scandalous set of gestures, he brushes his hand
against my arm and drapes an arm casually around my shoulder and
leans in when he speaks and leans in when I speak, all the better for
us both to hear.

And we continue talking in a dimly lit bar during the third and
last installment of the party, the one that signals the end is near. We
talk so much and so easily that I feel an uncharacteristic confidence
rising in me, a confidence that says something as old as the ages will
happen tonight, that this something has been simmering for a very
long time now.

After all, we have not only been talking tonight but have been
talking a great deal in *public*, and in a crowd that's watching our
every move, and I know that in Japan this counts for something, this
public display of interest, though I'm not entirely sure what this something is.

We talk about books, what writers we like, what writers we don't;
we talk about our dreams, which we both admit involve writing and
which dominate our thoughts, though it scares us to think we might
never get serious enough.

I hope one day Marilyn-sensei writes a book, he says.

I nod as he talks but can't imagine such a thing. Because writing
a book seems like one of those things only a grown-up or someone
really, really smart could do and I don't feel like a grown-up yet and
I don't think I'm smart because I lack common sense. I left my oven
on once for two days running, after all. And anyway, writing a book
is something that might take place in the mythical future and to me,

right now, the only future I can think about is tonight, what will happen when we leave this bar.

Right now in this smoky bar, I am thinking about what's here. How Nozaki is sitting here next to me, how he is telling me he can imagine me one day writing a book and I am telling him, *Yes, writing a book would be great, though it also sounds awfully hard, but why stop with that? Why stop with a book?*

He should also hope to hear that I am blissfully and happily and amazingly married and living in some small white stucco house with polished hardwood floors and tall windows that miraculously remain clean and tiny bedrooms on the second floor where we tuck the children, a boy and a girl, into bed, the boy with red hair, the girl with black hair, and between our legs run two fat and happy cats, Violet and Sherman, named because the children loved the names Violet and Sherman and we never knew why, we couldn't find out why but we said, if they love the names then that will be that. And outside our house with its fat happy cats will be a garden and the garden will be filled with tomatoes and basil and parsley and mint and flowers, too, flowers like lilies and irises and daisies and also many different kinds of trees, including slender bamboo trees and also one enormous blue spruce. And near our house, a few miles away, is the ocean and we will love the ocean for its gorgeous gray and craggy-rocked beach and also for the fact that we cannot see it from our house, that, like so many things, it remains always slightly out of reach.

He should want for me to *have it all*, I say, including and especially ordinary love, which never seemed anything less than extraordinary to me.

He laughs at the extravagance of my dreams, then says no, he hopes only that Marilyn-san will write a book one day. *Because marriage is ordinary but writing a book is not.*

And then it is closing time and the businessmen are dozing off and not even the prospect of flirting with a hostess or ordering more whiskey seems likely to keep anyone awake and Nozaki and I are still going strong, it feels like we're just getting started. *They're your guys*, I whisper this to him, confident he will do something to orchestrate all that will happen next. *Do what you have to do to get rid of them.*

And miraculously he does, saying something to the businessmen in Japanese that I can't quite make out, maybe that he will make sure that

Marilyn-sensei gets home safely in a taxi, that the others don't have to worry about seeing Marilyn-san gets home.

Then they're gone — poof! — and we leave the bar too and Nozaki leads me by the arm toward the only place in Shiojiri still open at that late hour: A Taiwanese hostess bar where we continue talking over coffee, after which, we walk to his office where we sit close and continue talking some more, easily and happily and I am remembering something he said once during class, in a lesson where I asked each businessman to use the rooms of a house to tell a story about himself. Nozaki said, *I usually make love in the bedroom but I want to make love in the kitchen* and I had complimented him on such a sturdy, grammatically correct little sentence and also the flair with which he told a sentence-length story.

I'm thinking what his kitchen might look like, what his bedroom might look like, whether he's a careful housekeeper or messy as can be, and then finally, finally, finally, when I can't stand it anymore, I lean in and say, *Aren't you going to kiss me sometime soon?* and I have that vague sensation that the negative construction of my sentence may be too complicated to understand but I am too happy and too drunk to know how to uncomplicate that and happily, he reads my body, he makes his way through the mess of my words, he answers my question with a kiss and the kiss is perfect, the kiss is not chaste, and now I am not thinking of anything right now. I close my eyes and let nature take nature's natural course, my whole body smiling as Nozaki takes charge, starts circling his hands around my shoulders, starts pulling me into his body, close.

And if I were? If my mind were composing any sentences at all?

I would be thinking, *This is why a woman travels. For this.*

Later that night, we drive to a love motel because Nozaki says I should see one before I leave Japan and I am charmed that he wants me to see such a thing, then surprised that the motel looks so completely ordinary, just like an ordinary hotel except that there is a laundry chute-style cubby hole in one wall where you can pay the bill discreetly, as if you were depositing money at a drive-through bank without having to see a clerk face to face.

When the moon starts to fade and the sun starts to rise and we can't see any of this because we are falling asleep, both of us too tired to undress, too tired to do anything but fall into the big double bed, I ask Nozaki what took him so long, why he waited till now, till the night of my farewell party, to do something, to make a move.

His arm is around my neck, my leg is curled around his, and I am marveling that it has finally come to this, that we are, finally, touching, even though it's only through our clothes. And he tells me he waited because Nozaki-san was very, very shy, and he had been too embarrassed to speak to Marilyn-*sensei* until tonight and his English, he knows, is very, very poor. And then, in what sounds like perfect English to me, he says the words I didn't know I had been waiting to hear.

For a long time, I hoped for this situation, and I smile, kissing his handsome ear.

know an American woman who studied mime in Paris for many years. The city, she says, smelled like piss. The trick to miming, she says, is not what you'd think. You don't *visualize* the object of the imagination — the ball, the brick wall, the flower to bloom for the small, dark-haired girl on the front row, the girl waiting in her velvet dress — but *imagine* the weight of the object, feel the weight as if it were real.

What happens next happens as if out of time and space. The time is spring. The place is Japan. The woman is me. Nozaki is the man. These are the facts. But why is it facts never seem like enough? What I want to remember is not meeting the men but the feeling after. The weight involved. The weight of affection. I remember that.

I remember meeting Nozaki in bar after bar, the beer always bitter, the food always fine. I remember that small kitchen of his. Perfect pears, ripe tomatoes, bracing *soba* noodles. I remember drinking wine made from Shiojiri grapes.

I remember the struggle of communicating as if the struggle mattered more than the words themselves. I remember gliding along in the cloud of his big white car. Where we were going — I never cared where.

What do you see? Nozaki asks one night as we drive. *What do you see when you look at the moon?*

It has never occurred to me that the moon is more than the moon. *Nothing,* I say. Just the moon. *Why? What do you see?*

A rabbit, he says, braking at a red light.

I glance out the window at *pachinko* parlors passing by, at the *ramen* shops with steam rising from their tops, at the rice fields and cemeteries, before looking back at Nozaki's face and I think what a wonder it is, this face, this night, and this trick of a man pulling a rabbit out of a moon.

I lean in to try to read his lips in the dark. If I can watch as well as listen, there's a better chance I will understand. Tonight he is driving and asking about Iowa, the dreamy place I will live in the fall. The school that has accepted me.

Was it difficult to get in?

I don't know, I answer truthfully, *but since I made it, I have to doubt it, ne?*

I ask him about his college days. He majored in law at a university in Tokyo but always wanted and planned to write. He was afraid he wouldn't be able to make a living as a writer, but now, with all the legal work he has — he is the only lawyer for miles around — he finds little time to try.

He took the test required to practice law ten times before passing.

The average, he says, *is nine.*

But I challenged, he continues, and I smile, knowing the word he means is *persevered.* Passing the test required ninety-nine percent hard work and one percent luck.

I'm glad I learned my Japanese numbers now.

I look at him in the dark of the car, his slick black hair flecked with strands of gray, his slight but handsome frame.

You are my one percent, I do not say.

O ne night, Nozaki and I sit on the stairs that lead from his law office on ground level to his apartment above and we talk about our respective jobs.

Nozaki's black cat saunters by, pauses by her master, then arches her back, hisses and storms past me, her *neko* nose high and haughty in the air.

She is only jealous, Nozaki says when I ask if it's something I said. I am pleased by this, that there is something for Miss Kitty to be jealous about, but also just a little stung. No cat has ever rejected me before.

I ask Nozaki about the cases he worked on today and he says they are too boring to talk about.

He asks me about my job at the ABC School and when I tell him I like it, no, that I *love* this job, he raises his eyebrows, says, *Marilyn-sensei is a teacher for adults.*

I ask him what he means by that and he says he thinks I am too smart to teach babies, that the job is too simple for an intelligent woman to enjoy for long.

I am flattered, I say, *but you are wrong about this.* I love working at the ABC School, love teaching the toddlers songs like "I'm Mad at You," love working out puzzles with teenagers, creating treasure hunts that take them all over town. I love getting tiny glimpses into the lives of the adult students. One day a woman, taking English classes to prepare for her first trip abroad, tells me about the most difficult time in her life, a time when her children were small and her husband was never home. She speaks of her husband's "accidents" in those days. Only later do I realize by "accidents" she means "affairs."

I love the routines of the school, the way repetition provides relief from the chaos in my head. I love the simplicity of the classroom, which provides a respite from a life now dominated by men. I love the books we use, the pictures that pose questions in rhyme: *Can you feel the wind? Can you touch the stars? Can you see their lovely light? Can you see the moon in the afternoon? Can you touch the stars at night?*

We use a program at the ABC School that relies on a quick review of vocabulary through flashcards. As the instructor, I am supposed to add more difficult words to the pile each week and then, through flashcards, ask students to review easier ones in quick succession to reinforce what they already know.

Most of the cards are easy to figure out. Pictures of oranges and apples and bananas in the pile labeled *fruit.* A living room, a kitchen, a bathroom, and a bedroom in pictures called *rooms of a house.* Or pictures delineating those troublesome little particles such as *on* and *under,* all of which have the words written on the back as a teacher's cheat sheet.

A few of the cards, though, are missing those answers on the back. They leave me wondering what the makers of the system had in mind. In a pile of cards labeled *nouns,* for instance, is a picture of a girl holding a pencil in the air, close to her ear. Every time I see the card, I go blank as to what the cue is supposed to be, and I find myself giggling as I tell the kids to repeat after me,

You have a pencil in your ear, I say. *Please repeat.*

You have a pencil in your ear, they say straight-faced, in unison. I wonder if they're being polite or are just happily unaware.

I love the mystery of why a woman has a pencil in her ear. And I love working late into the night at the ABC School, making birthday cards for the children after all the classes are done, after all the other teachers have gone. I love cutting out construction paper constellations of suns and moons and stars and placing these papery worlds onto the walls, next to flash cards with questions written in big black block letters, the kind too clear for anyone to misread: *When is your birthday? Do you like cats? Can fish fly?* I love wondering, *Can fish fly?* It seems possible. Anything seems possible.

I look at Nozaki and wonder how to tell him this.

I DO, I say. *I love the ABC School. I could happily live here and work at the ABC School every day.*

But Nozaki shakes his head, looks skeptical still. My legs are cramped here, sitting on the stairs. I wish I were brave; I would sing a teasing version of "I'm Mad at You" to him.

Nozaki smiles. *Marilyn-san will teach adults one day.*

I shrug and reach for the kitty who jumps away. I say, *Who knows what either one of us will one day do.*

ne night, all the bars in Matsumoto are full so we weave our way to the town's sole expatriate bar. At Scotty's I order beers in English while Nozaki waits. It's different with me in charge. Usually Nozaki negotiates all our eating and drinking in Japanese. When our beers arrive, I forget where I am—the country of Japan—and drink straight from the bottle rather than pouring the beer into glasses—first for him, then for me—as I usually would. Nozaki watches, his eyes getting wide.

What? I ask.

It's just very strange to see a woman drink beer like that.

I ask Nozaki if he dislikes this, the sight of a woman drinking from the bottle as I am now and he says no and part of me believes him but part of me wonders, what does he see? On some level is he repelled? Aroused? Curious? Some combination of all three? He's told me before that he does not take cultural habits too seriously, that he believes a person can be American or Japanese but have more in common with someone French, Brazilian or Sudanese. But it's never the theoretical I care about with him; it's always the personal, the naggingly personal. I don't wonder right now about ideas. I wonder what he thinks of *me*.

We continue drinking. I order two more beers. Nozaki tells me that he thinks the most honorable life is a life lived simply, that he has a fantasy of himself as a farmer in old age, and as this farmer he will—how do you say it?—*cultivate* fresh vegetables from the ground, and as he talks I realize I am loving this, loving the night, the conversation, the word "cultivate"—*tagayasu*—that saturates my sense of everything and now that I have heard Nozaki's fantasy of old age, I am devising one of my own, thinking I want to be a farmer's wife and I like this idea, secretly convincing myself that this is what I've always longed to be, a farmer's wife, fat and frumpy, happy with her stout radish legs, content to live a simple life that revolves around raising vegetables and making for herself at midday—for this is a time of day she relishes for its privacy—a strong cup of Japanese tea.

And before all that? Before our lives on this farm begin? Before that, I imagine, we will live a life of ordinary joy, the kind that has always eluded me. First Nozaki will come to Iowa to visit. He will marvel at the sight of the prairie and sigh at the size of that wide Midwestern sky. He will smile when we walk past all those cheerful Iowa houses with their red geraniums growing in pots on wide front porches.

And then he will return to his home in Japan and he will study English, and in Iowa I will get serious about tackling Japanese, learning to read the *kanji* beyond "man" and "woman" and "apple" and "child." And eventually, I will return to Japan to be with Nozaki, to make our new home there—*here*—and he will continue working every day at the law practice underneath his apartment and I will go to work at the little ABC School that I love and we will have a little plot of land nearby where we will grow radishes, tomatoes, peppers and corn, and we will go along, happily, meeting up after work in his messy little apartment, his *crazy place*, as he calls it, only by then, I will have cleaned it up and imposed some sense of order, put the books onto tidy cedar bookshelves, organized his clothes, and put away mine, everything into its proper place, and then I will arrange red tulips on the table in a clear square vase. And in the kitchen at night we will cook dinners of fish with salad and rice and it's here that in that crazy place, this little kitchen, this room that's cleaned up in my mind's eye, it's here that we will raise a couple of kids, a red-haired, brown-eyed boy and a black-haired, blue-eyed girl, children who, because of their parents, will speak two languages or some beautiful and eccentric mix, pidgin-speak peppered by the kind of private vocabulary every family constructs.

Apples wasuki desu ka?

Does okaa-san like persimmon fruit?

Pass the gohan, please, ne?

And in my mind, the picture is so lovely that I imagine we will even have a pigeon or two as pets, all of us, creatures in a life brushed, like the mysterious *kanji* I cannot read, by some measure of grace.

I imagine all this at Scotty's before I have finished my second beer.

Then Nozaki says, *What is Marilyn-san thinking about?* and I say, *Nothing. Everything. Nozaki-san. Love.* I smile and ask him if he has a philosophy of love and he says yes.

Love is wide, he says, and by *wide* I know that he means *big* because all the time I hear Japanese people say, *American houses are very wide,* by which I know they mean *American houses are very big.* And the word seems right and the world does too, very fragile, yes, and delicate and small, but a portal through which I see something large and impressive.

Who was the famous biologist who said it was human nature to appreciate a view?

I smile and Nozaki smiles back and I notice for the first time that his teeth are crooked and gray and I think these crooked gray teeth, they are beautiful and I could watch them every day.

What? he says.

I must be smiling like a lunatic.

What? he says. His voice is urgent now.

Nothing, I say, *it's nothing. It's just that I like to listen to you.*

My eyes have filled with tears, he can see, and I brush them away and say, *honest it's nothing,* because it's starting again, I'm starting to cry at unpredictable times just as I did years ago at home in my almost-perfect life, and the tears are part of something again, something that I cannot even begin to explain again, and there's a change coming, I can count on that, and I'm still smiling wide, still smiling big like a woman madly in love, like the madwoman I was meant to be, and I pick up my bottle of Sapporo beer and raise it high, saying, *Kampai* and *cheers!*

Love *is* wide, I think, looking back now through the lens of love and memory and many years. *Love is wide.*

The men in my country smoke too much. On trains, in restaurants, at temples, at home in the middle of the night — they reach for cigarettes first thing in the morning, before they eat breakfast, before they drink coffee, before they have kissed the women they claim to love, the women who sleep so quietly, who never smoke.

The men in my country sleep too much. They sleep on trains, at bus stops, in cars, in meetings. They sleep, I think, because they work so hard. They study too much. They drink too much. Too much *sake* and whiskey and way too much beer, which, in those tiny glasses, one after another, adds up.

They study and work and drink and go without sleep, looking worn-out, bone-tired, ready to collapse in a heap.

The men in my country have black-black hair. And skin as smooth as a baby's. They wear dark suits and white shirts and skinny dark ties that make them look like actors in a black and white film. They are a sober bunch. They are sober even when down-and-out drunk. And they so rarely smile that when they do, it is hard not to feel as if something miraculous just occurred, that such a smile could only mean one thing, that they're in love, that these men are in love.

The men in my country begin with Nozaki and end with Nozaki and circle back to Nozaki. And these are things I observe before meeting Nozaki so that in meeting him, the country and the man become entwined. These are the things I observe in the country that belongs to Nozaki, the country that I want to be mine.

One night, at a Mediterranean restaurant, Nozaki orders scallops and green salad and coffee and dessert. It is strange but good to be eating in a place where all the food is out on the table open-faced instead of covered up in small secret dishes, Japanese style, so good that I eat with great gusto, the scallops and the salad, all of it, and then, only then realize that the waitress has put the plate of greens on the table for both of us to share.

Why didn't you tell me? I ask him. *Why didn't you say something?* Nozaki pours me another glass of wine, shrugs in that offhand way I like, and says he thought it was *Marilyn-san's style*, that's all, and the way he says it — using my name as is customary here instead of the pronoun *you* — makes me relax, third person distancing me from my crime.

We drive, we eat, we cook, and we go to see films. One night in Matsumoto, we find that the twenty-four-hour parking garage where we parked his car earlier closed at midnight when we thought it would stay open till 2 A.M. It is 1 A.M. now. A taxi to Nozaki's place would cost a small fortune from here. So I suggest we take a taxi to Sara's house nearby, where I sometimes sleep in her extra room.

Sara's another teacher at the ABC School. She rents a small cottage from the Nozawa family, one that their parents will take over when they are old. We have to go through the family's small yard to get to Sara's cottage. Nozaki and I whisper as we open the gate, walking quietly over loose garden steps. But before I open the door, the family dog starts barking from inside the Nozawa's house and won't settle down. It is dark and I can't see Nozaki's face but I can tell he's nervous, thinks this was a bad idea.

The dog barks at everyone, I whisper. *Don't worry. It'll be OK.*

In the spare room, we take the length of borrowed futons and Nozaki looks around at my belongings, minimal now, since I've boxed up and shipped most of my worldly items back to the United States. I have only a few books, a few clothes, a few dishes and CDs left and they're split up between two places: here and the spare room at Natsume-san's house.

Marilyn-san is very neat, he says, and I am pleased by this, pleased beyond belief.

We talk about music, novels, taste. We talk about the businessmen, people we both know, comparing notes. When I tell Nozaki that I like Mori-san, that Mori-san always manages to make me laugh, Nozaki frowns and says that Mori-san's sense of humor is underdeveloped and young.

Of course, I say. But I hold my ground, recognize this for what it is. *To me you are the most handsome and the funniest and the kindest and most intelligent and ichiban of all. Still, I LIKE Mori-san, too. He makes me smile.*

Nozaki's face softens, his jealousy drifting away. Yes, he admits, he likes Mori-san too.

He looks tired right now, after all this talk, and I am too. I ask him if he'd like go to sleep.

No, he says. *This is —*

I can't understand the word he has used.

He looks it up in the bright green dictionary I keep within reach, points at a word and hands the book to me.

Valuable.

I nod. This is valuable to me as well.

Sometimes I try to imagine what it would be like to talk to Nozaki in Japanese, to rattle off a complicated idea or make a joke that relies on word play. I try to imagine creating in high speed with lots of big words some detailed scene from my past. I try to imagine describing those things I think about: the lines of my mother's face, which I so often miss; the flatness of the land I imagine Iowa will be; the thrill of buying a bouquet of freshly cut tulips each week, tulips I put on the front desk at the cheerful ABC School next to the crayoned self-portraits of the toddlers who are students there.

I can't talk that way, the way I would at home, can't even come close. And neither can he. But I think maybe I like our way best. Talk as seductive as a stroll on the beach, languid and luxurious as if we had all the time in the world.

On the futons, Nozaki kisses, then touches me, and all at once I begin to cry. He asks what's wrong, and I tell him I don't know.

I'm sorry, I say, but I *don't* know.

He holds me for a while, strokes my hair, and then, a few minutes later I tell him in a mix of two tongues, *First time . . . hajimete. Feeling in my heart is . . . strong. When we're together, feeling — the first time, ne?*

The other men — the professor and Amir — seem far away.

Nozaki laughs, puts his arms around me again and holds me that way all night long.

Only later do I wonder if what I said was true.

I know so few Japanese words that I tend to use the ones that are most familiar to me. Maybe these words, the few right on the tip of my tongue, precede emotion and define what is only barely there. Maybe this is why words matter so much. Because they turn the abstract into something concrete, defining and surprising you when they turn a flutter of the heart into something tangible and real.

The question with Amir winds up being practical and pure: Where can we go to be alone? When I took the job at the ABC School and moved out of my teachers' flat, owned by the city, I became a vagabond without a place to call her own, moving between Natsume-san's house and Sara's borrowed extra room.

Amir's place, where he lives, is too crowded with his housemates from Iran. I cannot bring him to Natsume-san's house. We go to Sara's sometime but we agree it doesn't quite feel right.

And so we find ourselves sneaking all over town instead, going to parks, to temples, to friends' apartments when those friends are out of town, all of this to touch each other in every conceivable illicit place, on grassy patches, on castle grounds and underneath the bright red of these cities' Shinto shrines, near the altars of the Buddhist temples, in parks and on park benches, touching so much and so often that finally all that touch, it wears us out, it begins to wear thin and all we want, all we crave, we admit one night, is the comfort of sharing a private bed.

And so, one night I usher Amir back into the apartment that used to be mine, the one that we used to cook in and bathe in, the one where, a few months ago when we hardly knew each other, he sat me on a chair one night, arranging to cut my hair, leaning in close, all concentration, and I remember he smelled like soap. The apartment, I know, will remain vacant for a few months until a new American teacher is scheduled to move in. No electricity but the place still has its cache of supplies — running water; futons in the closet; kerosene in the kerosene heater; the heater still sitting there right on the floor.

And so, we slip into this place during the thick folds of night, quietly removing our shoes in the *genkan*, hoping the neighbors won't hear us gliding across *tatami* mats in our stocking feet, shadows now to each other, ghostly sights.

Amir lights the kerosene heater. I slide open the closet door and pull the futons down quietly. We arrange ourselves and bedding on the floor and fall asleep, too tired to touch.

Slip out before dawn.

Return again and again.

One night we consider cooking dinner on top of that kerosene heater in the room that no longer belongs to me but we think better of it. Instead Amir ducks out to a nearby 7-Eleven and returns with two microwave-heated *bentō* boxes of chicken balls and rice. We eat that night by the light of our kerosene moon, whispering for fear the neighbors will hear us — who knows what will happen then — and in my memory the meal is the most delicious of any I've ever had.

This is the night that, after dinner, Amir tells me fragments of his Iranian past, how he fought in the Army, how this isn't something he likes to think about anymore, unless someone asks. It is late now. The glow from the kerosene heater has turned the room into a candlelit church and Amir whispers, *Are you sleepy yet?*

No, I whisper. I'm wide awake. How strange it is, I think, to lie near someone so gentle, knowing he has killed men in a war somewhere. And how lucky we are to have met on neutral turf, a place far away from both of our homes, miles away from competing political ideologies that might, at another time and in another place, make it impossible for us to be together like this.

I'm trying to take care, to cherish what goes on between us but never confuse it for something it is not. Amir, I know, does the same.

Like is once a week, he tells me just before we both fall asleep, the talk having turned from war to the nature of love. *Love every day.*

ne morning I meet the professor for coffee and ask him if he ever worries about being seen in public with me.

I am sure that he will say that he is but that he wants to see me so badly that he just doesn't care, that he's willing to take risks.

What he says next surprises me.

No, I do not worry. No Japanese would ever imagine I am having an affair with you.

When he drives me back to the ABC School that day, I'm reeling from what I think of as the greatest of put-downs. I script mine to throw back at him, telling the professor he reminds me of Mr. Kato, one of the Japanese businessmen. Mr. Kato, the professor knows, is someone who brags about his routine extramarital affairs and I have said before that I pity him.

The professor looks stunned, then hurt, then mad.

These emotions pass like shadows across the professor's face and I'm thrilled at the power I have to sting him back. Then the bite of power fades as the professor says in a way that makes my whole body ache, *This is my first. And surely when you leave, this will be my last.*

saw an exhibit in a Chicago art museum once that featured the
work of the American photographer Harry Callahan: black and
white studies of nature and the female form. Black and white
studies of the sensual slope of grass. Black and white curves of
a woman's back, of Eleanor, Callahan's wife.

This, I thought, *is how desire looks.*

In a video accompanying the exhibit, Callahan said that at
one time he had paid attention to what the critics said about his work.
Listened, for instance, to their observation that he was obsessed with
lines. And so, as an experiment, he gave into that observation and
began playing with lines, cutting up small pieces of black thread and
arranging them against a plain white backdrop.

But the project bored him.

What he was interested in, he said, was not line, but Eleanor. And
grass.

One Sunday afternoon Nozaki surprises me by suggesting we visit
Gofukuji, a Buddhist temple on a high beautiful hill, and as we
do, as we climb the steps to the temple, he surprises me further by
asking Marilyn-san questions about what she considers the meaning
of life.

Ask me that after dark, I say. *It's too early to talk about existentialism or
life or fate or will.*

But he presses. We are breathless now, only beginning our way up
all these stairs. There must be more than a hundred of them.

What about for you?

I'm trying to stall to gather my thoughts. Our conversations feel
loaded from the start, serious in a way that others never are. I wonder

why that is. Because of who we are? A man and a woman? Two people in their thirties, on the brink of middle age? Japanese and American? Is this the category that defines us now?

We have no models to work from, no public images shimmering in the distance. When I walk down the streets of Roppongi in Tokyo and look at American men holding hands with Japanese women, the couples seem charmed, straight out of the script of a World War II film, the men benevolent dictators of sorts, the women some variation of exotic, forbidden female fruit. People aren't as simple as this and I know my reaction is reductive, unfair. Still, I wonder. Does he see in her some feminine ideal? Does she see masculine perfection in him? I imagine they walk with a bearing that suggests they never wonder if they fit in.

Nozaki and I, on the other hand, seem hunched over when we walk. And without examples of *gaijin* women with Japanese men, I think we are working without a net. Or maybe that's some high-minded excuse I want to give us. An out. To say that we are going it alone, culturally speaking, when really, in my heart of hearts I suspect it's more fundamental than that. Maybe we are two people who would rather be alone.

A line from Leonardo da Vinci floats in and out of my mind.

Every luminous body grows larger as it becomes more remote.

What the moon is. What Nozaki is.

I remember a game we played over coffee at Royal Host a few weeks ago.

Say whatever you think of first, I told him. *Whatever words you think of when you think of me.*

I wanted to test the waters, to find out how he felt about me and how conscious he was of my nationality. I was sure that if he said *American* I would know that he was involved with me because I am a *gaijin*, not because of me-me. But that's not what happened. That's not what he revealed at all.

Pretty, he said. *Woman. Gentle. Smart.*

I was stunned by the list, flattered beyond belief.

No one has ever said these things to me.

I feared a punch line was coming, that I would find out he was playing a joke.

Then the game ended when he said *teacher*, and I hit him on the arm in mock disapproval, reminding him that the conversation class ended a long time ago, that I wasn't his teacher anymore, that I would never be his teacher again.

Today, as we reach the top of the stairs and approach the temple, I wonder what would make my list about him. All the usuals, no doubt, all the clichés, all the things everyone in love claims and believes are the beloved's unique attributes. *Smart. Handsome. Complicated. Sweet.*

And a few more. *Confusing. Compelling. Tender. Remote.*

And this, a phrase I cannot censor, nor one I can say I understand: *The one who will change me.*

That's what he is. And that's what I'm thinking as we come to the temple, Nozaki's question still hanging in the air.

What is life about for you?

To think, he says. That is what his life is about.

I remember now having visited this temple before, having come here with a teacher from school. The teacher introduced me to the priest, who stopped whatever his priestly duties were for the day to sit with us and to have a cup of tea.

The priest's shaved head reminded me of a swimmer. He wore a long black robe and carried prayer beads that looked like a candy necklace to me, something I had the urge to lick. He told us about the history of the temple and a special statue of Buddha brought out once every thirty-three years. And in the background there was incense and the meeting seemed intoxicating to me, especially when the priest reached inside his deep black robe and willy-nilly, out spilled a pack of cigarettes.

The men in my country smoke too much.

And think too much.

And remain as distant and lovely as the moon.

I know my answer to his question.

To love, I think, but I refuse to say so out loud here and now.

We have reached the top of the stairs and can see the temple now with its clean spare lines and its old thatched roof. We will drink from the temple's fountain. I will say a silent prayer.

To love a foreign man. To stay in Japan. That's my answer.

And to watch your luminosity grow.

The professor continues calling. I continue calling him back. We continue meeting and I see that, as neither mistress nor friend, I occupy some peculiar in-between place in the professor's life. And I begin to think of us as two people stuck on some terrible borderline, a place where ordinary restrictions no longer apply but where ordinary pleasures, too, cease to exist.

One morning we meet for coffee, only I have a bad cold, so I order tea. The professor starts in on his monologue. Tells me he believes in marriage as a social and legal institution. I start to roll my eyes. I have heard this several times before. But then he adds something new: that he thinks it's a crime to change in marriage, as he observes so many Japanese men so often do.

What do you mean? I ask.

Only that men, once they have pushed to marry, begin looking elsewhere and pulling away.

Instead of telling him this phenomenon is not exactly Japanese, I cut to the chase, mix things up gender-wise.

You mean the way your first wife did?

His first wife and her infidelity — the professor brought her up once when we first met but she isn't someone we have talked about since.

Yes, he says, looking me in the eye.

And suddenly I feel sorry for what I have just said, what I've made him do, how I have forced him to publicly acknowledge a betrayal in his life. My head hurts. My hands instinctively reach for the cup of hot tea.

But now that I've started, I see no way out. I have opened this particular can of worms. Now I can't very well turn away and pretend the worms aren't there, crawling between us, into our coffee cups and down our throats.

I continue. *And how have I affected your marriage?* For I know, not out of vanity, that I have. The professor, after all, has affected me, though this, too, is something we don't discuss: the way I see the professor preparing me for Amir, and Amir leading to Nozaki, the way these relationships can't be separated into neat little piles of nouns like those on flashcards at the ABC School.

The fact is, the men are all mixed up together, the thread of one running into another, the threads of all three part of the country itself, and all in a way that, for a long time afterward I will try to untangle in my mind. We are in each other's lives, yet the professor and I rarely talk about this, the mix and the mess, because doing so would require facing up to this: that Nozaki is to me what I am to the professor, a modern miracle, that rare and unexpected find.

When you showed up in my life, I started noticing things in my marriage, the professor says. *These things have been both good and bad.*

So now you are changing in your marriage? I say. *Now you are committing the crime?*

The professor is stunned into silence, then tells me I'm more brilliant than usual when sick. And I think, OK, this is how it's going to be: we'll trade insight for flattery. I smile in thanks. And the worms recede, slipping back into the table of wood.

Sometimes we rise above the cycle, pull ourselves out of the quicksand before the thickness of words drags us down.

Sometimes the professor is so open, so vulnerable, that listening to him breaks my heart.

What's new? I ask him one day at Royal Host.

Nothing, he says and I can hear a familiar melancholy in his voice, the kind that reminds me of my own, the kind that binds us, keeping us unhappily close.

Come on, I press. *Surely there's something new on your mind.*

No, he says, and I know to back off.

I have, he continues, in a voice that's honest and sad and undeniably resigned, *an ordinary life.*

One ordinary day, we decide to go out to the country for a drive. His car is as neat as a pin, as neat as his office at school, and I find myself craving a disruption of virtue, some sign of dirt, something misplaced:

a gum wrapper on the floor, a child's sun hat left on the dash, a stack of student papers on the back seat — something, anything, some sign of life.

Within minutes after having buckled myself in, I realize this drive is a bad idea in more ways than one. For the professor drives in such a stop-start way, riding the brake as if he is trying to stop us from sliding on ice, that I can feel myself starting to get sick.

Have you ever driven on Japanese roads? he asks.

No, I say, *I don't have an international driver's license. Why?*

I only wondered.

I smile at him and his desire to make small talks, then tell him, *I think maybe I'm getting sick.*

Shall I stop the car? he asks.

Not yet.

And for the next few minutes as the professor drives, I linger in that in-between state, not quite well and not quite sick. Then something nasty rises in my throat and I tell the professor maybe now might be a good time to pull over, if he doesn't mind.

He stops the car next to an open field of yellow flowers and I get out of the car and walk down a quiet residential street, breathing in the country air, just breathing deeply, trying to keep my head still. We are out in the country but the country still looks crowded here, lots of houses yards apart, not on top of one another like in the city, and the air doesn't feel that fresh and I'm remembering something a Japanese teacher at school said once: that it was too bad, the pollution in Japan, all the *exhausted fumes* from cars.

When my stomach settles and my head begins to clear, I stop and turn and look back at the professor, standing by the car. He looks as if he has been watching me all along, a look of concern and worry on his face, and I wonder if anyone will ever look after me like that again.

The professor called me his miracle once. That was the word he used. His *miracle.*

I remained very still when he said this.

We were parked in his car by the side of a dark road.

His miracle. His first. His last.

Japan is an earnest country and the professor an honest man. When he used the word, the speaking made it so. And that night, I thought

I understood something about the nature of language and love, how they feed one another, how without one, the other will die. And also, paradoxically, how in silence, too, love may suffer but also thrive.

Someone drove by our car that night and the headlights from the car hit us, bathing us in a flash of white light where we sat in the front seat. He held my hand and said it would be okay, and even though I hadn't been scared, I found myself believing him anyway, believing we might not have been OK but now we would be, believing he was right. Instinctively, I turned my eyes away from the headlights of that passing car, lowering my head into the darkness of his shirt, taking him in, as an animal might, smelling him, marking him not as my own exactly but something else — the first of something I would never quite be able to pronounce.

Hajimete. First time.

A fleeting and fragile and tender place.

read about scientists once, who, in studying deer mice, found that in taking the small creatures out of their nest boxes at night, the mice were quick to return home to their nests, their boxes, on their own. But when the scientists returned the deer mice to their homes by hand, the mice were quick to try to leave once again, causing the scientists to conclude the mice cared less about comfort than the freedom of choice.

I've often wondered, though, if another study had followed, one in which the mice were given choice after choice every night of the week. Would the crushing consequence of choice have revealed itself? Would there come some point when desire for choice backfired? When the comfort of limited options kicked back in?

By mid-May, not even two months into juggling three men in my life, the men have become too much. I put Amir off for a week, telling him I can't see him, only to cave in to tell him we can get together but we can't have sex ever again.

Just once more? he asks over the phone.

I am flattered, but firm.

We meet at Sara's house one night when I know she won't be home. We stretch out on futons in absence of a couch. Amir's stomach begins to grumble, a low but persistent hum, and he laughs when I ask him, *Are you hungry?* because we both know he's not.

It's a mystery, he says. *My stomach speaks only when it sees you.*

And then, jokes out of the way, we begin to kiss and I wonder how I thought earlier I might resist when here is Amir, sweet and sunny, here is Amir on this cool spring night, here is Amir saving me the way only touch can: from the disaster of living solely for oneself.

Once I asked Amir about his past affairs. We had had a lot of sex by then or a lot of sex by my standards, anyway, which probably isn't saying all that much. And the sex had been so good and so easy, such a rare combination of raunchy and sweet, that I convinced myself he must be a player, that this is what he did all the time, that what happened between us couldn't be unusual, let alone unique.

How many? I had asked, hoping he understood I was not jealous, exactly, just curious about his past. He was twenty-seven years old; surely the number of past lovers might be high.

Four, he said, *and that includes you.*

No way, I said, punching him lightly on the chest.

But the look on Amir's face told me he was telling the truth.

Hontō ni? Really?

He nodded to answer yes.

Then how, I asked, *are you so skilled, so jōzu ne?*

He looked at me as if checking to see if I might be teasing him, and then, when it was clear I was serious, he became serious, too, and he thought for a minute and said he didn't know but that he thought maybe it was that he liked to listen to a woman's body, teaching himself to hear what a woman might want.

At Sara's, Amir is listening once again when I stop the kissing, stop to tell him I'm serious, I can't be with him like that, not now, not ever again.

I can't, I say. After all, I love another man.

Then, to protect myself, I rush from the bedroom to the living room where, at a distance from Amir, I plop down on a cushion, arms folded across my chest, mouth curled into a frown. If I could stand outside of myself, what I would see is a petulant child trapped in a woman's body, someone weeping in confusion because she's getting her way but not wanting it exactly. But because I don't live outside myself, because I live inside the petulant child's head, the tears seem natural, not part of some ploy.

Amir follows. Kneels down. Puts his arm around my shoulders and pulls me up, then leads me down through the hallway and back into our nest, our home. The wind whistles through a window someone broke before I came. And we fall back down again on the futons, his legs curled around mine, my head nestled in his neck. *It's okay,* he says, *it's okay.* His voice is a lullaby, his body a warm bed.

Amir never wanted sex only.

And to the sound of that syntax, we fall asleep.

A mir continues calling, usually just to check in and see how my day has gone, something I realize—and even now, years later, I find this both startling and sad—I have never before experienced with a man. And eventually, I recant on my earlier position, tell him it's okay to continue having sex.

Because the truth is, I love Amir. Not in the crazy, compelling way I love Nozaki, Nozaki who if I were thinking about this, which I'm not—not yet—hasn't been touching me much lately, has told me that sex for him is a mental thing. With Amir it's different. He makes me feel cared for, wanted, and it's the kind of care that doesn't damage anyone or exact some nasty psychic toll. Which is not to say we don't have our moments, arguments born of the most banal and jealous concerns.

Once, I meet a young American woman downtown who informs me she has met a friend of mine.

He asked me to give him English lessons, she tells me and I know before she says so, she is talking about Amir.

She is young—somewhere in her mid-twenties—blonde and blue-eyed and instantly I hate her because I fear what she will tell me about Amir and I hate her, too, because she's objectively cute. Because my reaction is ridiculous, I make up an excuse. I hate *bubbly* women, I tell myself, especially when these bubbly women are so young. So I hate her. Also, I don't trust her. Something tells me there's more than what she has already divulged.

I cut straight to the chase.

Did he come ON to you? I ask. I am dreading her answer, fearing she will say yes. This is the problem, I think, with a man who loves your body. If he loves your body, he will love other women's bodies too.

No, she says. *But . . .*

But what? I ask. I am beginning to feel woozy as if the Bubbly Girl had doused me with toxic champagne.

Nothing, really. Just a feeling. And . . .

And what?

And, I don't know. I guess I just haven't had such good luck with Middle Eastern men.

Oh, I say. That. Her comment confirms what I wanted confirmed: that this woman isn't worth Amir's or my time.

If you're the slightest bit uncomfortable, I tell her, hoping she won't see what I am now trying to do, *tell him no. I'm sure he'll understand.* I am pleased with myself for orchestrating this conversation to get what I want: information without revealing anything about myself.

Then this woman adds something innocuous as she leaves, something that leaves me seething all over again at absent Amir.

When they parted company, she says, flashing me her bubbly, insipid smile, he said this funny little thing. That *people are different everywhere*, so to *take care, always take care.*

Which is exactly what Amir has so often said to me. I had put stock in those words, infused them with meaning, inflated them with grace. He had ended nearly all of our conversations saying, *take care, take care* because *people are different everywhere*, his way, I had thought, of reminding me to be careful, to protect myself in the wide, unruly world, to remember that not everyone in the world could be trusted. And now, apparently, I should have been taking care against *him*.

Because here he is repeating these same words to her, the little linguistic cheat! And so, the next evening when I meet up with Amir, I am furious but determined to hide my fury and instead bristle proudly in a well-honed passive-aggressive way. Even Jesus was a doormat and a deity; even *He* found virtue in passive and aggressive means. If it was good enough for Christ Almighty, I think, it's damn well good enough for me today.

Amir and I walk from the train station toward a restaurant we both like. And on the way, Amir tries to make small talk about the weather, what a relief it is that it is finally spring, as he also tries to hold my hand and sing me a song, the kind he knows I like.

No *way*, I think, walking quickly ahead of him, folding my arms flat over my chest.

What's wrong? he asks.

And at first, I refuse to say. It would take a miracle, I think, for me to open up right now. But the walk is long and Amir looks so sweet. He seems genuinely perplexed by what must seem to him nothing more troubling than a bad mood. So finally, I relent.

I met a woman, I tell him, *who says she recently met Amir-san.*

And? he asks.

He doesn't seem to catch my drift. I am going to have to spell this out, and in a language borrowed for both of us.

You were FLIRTING with her, weren't you, I say, and we both know it's not a question. *Can you even IMAGINE how that makes me feel?*

I want to study ENGLISH, he says, *and as you've told me, you don't have all that much free time.*

We continue on, walking at a brisk and testy pace, arguing now in both English and Japanese, using a simple but jumbled and obviously angry mix.

But surely, I insist, *you had more than English in mind!*

Now he stops. Now he stares and we become two foreigners yelling at one another on the street, a caricature, no doubt, to anyone walking by.

I have never complained about Amir's other girlfriend, nor have I thought to question why three men aren't enough for me. But now, numbers are on my side. Numbers are my friends.

What, I screech. *Two women aren't enough for you?* I'm mad enough now that I don't give a rat's ass if he leaves. I begin walking again. If he stays or leaves, lives or dies—I have decided: I don't care, I don't give a shit.

Amir follows. Grabs me by the arm. Then becomes mad enough to retaliate in return.

Two women, he says, looking me straight in the eye, *are two too many right now.*

And the look on his face—he's clearly *baffled* by this—jolts me out of my jealous fit and we both burst out laughing and I slip out of my anger as if I were slipping out of a *yukata* for a bath and we walk to the restaurant holding hands, where Amir fixes me a salad from the salad bar with everything I want: tomatoes and croutons, no beans or alfalfa sprouts.

What surprises me with Amir are not the misunderstandings themselves but how quickly we work them out, and how good it feels to get the words and the feelings between us right.

Once when he has been out of town for the week, he calls me six times in a single day and at three different places — at Sara's, at Natsume-san's school, and at other friends' places, where I sometimes visit. When he finally tracks me down, I start crying, I am so happy to hear his voice.

I've missed you, I say, surprised as anyone at the tears, at the quick outpouring of relief.

Miss? he says, failing to understand. *Spell, please.*

But my attempts to do so only confuse him more since the only time Amir has heard "miss" has been in the context of titles, for Miss Sasaki or Miss Marilyn, as an honorific tag alongside Mr. Nozaki or Mr. Amir.

No, I MISS *you,* I say, wondering why we even try. Why bother to talk so much when talk only causes us to make mistakes, to misspeak? *Miss as in* HOMESICK. *Marilyn-san is homesick for her friend, Amir.*

Wakatta, he says. Now he understands. And the patience with which he listens, along with the pang of the truth — I *do* miss him — make me wonder all over again what's wrong with me that I don't crave the sun more than Nozaki's cool indirect light.

Here is Amir, always happy. Here is Amir who never fails to make me laugh. Here is Amir who touches me and who calls on the telephone to say, *Talk to me,* and when I say, *What about?* he says, *About yourself.*

And here is the truth: that every time we go through the routine, no matter how familiar, no matter how worn, those last two words always leave me moved.

One night I tell Amir I can't see him anymore, that sex or no sex, the situation has become too confusing for me, that some women can juggle several men at once, but I am not one of them, despite what recent actions suggest. He listens but says nothing. I press him by asking what he'd do tomorrow if I said that was it, that I couldn't see him again, period.

And very, very gently, he says, *I remember.*

And this, of course, is why I continue seeing Amir. Because he understands so well what I am only beginning to see. That remembering is the only way, finally, of keeping someone near.

live in the land of memory now, have remembered now for seven years.

I remember fragments, piled up.

The rustling of the trees. Laundry flapping in a breeze.

The curve of a river. Steps leading to a temple on the hill.

A girl next door practicing the violin at 8 o'clock every day.

An old man on the street, singing. A chant? A Buddhist prayer? I wondered for months, then learned he was selling octopus, fried.

I remember slips of the tongue, my own beautiful mistakes.

The man at a bar who leans in to say, *I'm leaving now.*

The woman who hears, *I need you and how.*

A drive to the country. No radio. Just small talk. Him saying *Kimochi ii* and me saying, what does that mean? Him saying, *the feeling is good,* and me saying, then *Kimochi ii* too.

I remember how Amir began practicing his English, not for me, he said, but as a gift to himself. He had learned Japanese quickly. I was sure he would learn English with similar ease. I gave him some old textbooks and one night in my kitchen, he wrote down in a notebook stray words and sentences he asked me to correct. His list reflected an odd mix of typical textbook fare—*What's Bill wearing?*—and phrases we had used between us—*Please wait for me.*

The list also included words out of context. *East. West. Memory. Drizzling.* And there were words I remember thinking sounded wonderful but far away, words I hadn't used in a long time, words that I later came to associate with him. *Jubilation,* for example, and *pineapples* and *rooftops* and *dawn.*

When Amir asked, *Do you like small trip?* I forgot he was practicing and answered, *Sure.* When he said, *You are very beautiful and kind,* I pushed and said, *Thank you very much*. He laughed and reminded me this was an English lesson, not real life.

But when he asked me to correct the sentence he composed—*If I be with you anytime I think I have all things*—I knew we had crossed some line.

I told him his English was beautiful, that he got the phrase exactly right.

And this, I remember this: How one night Amir invited me to dinner. How he lived in a flat above the noodle factory where he worked. His boss, a strict Japanese man, stayed late to do the books sometimes and wouldn't approve: a male worker bringing a woman home and me, a *gaijin*, a foreigner, an American at that. So Amir sneaks me in, whispering *hurry, please hurry*, as we rush through the dark hallway between job and home.

Once inside, there are his housemates, all polite, hard-working Iranian men, all in their twenties or early thirties, working in this country illegally, sending money home in plain Japanese envelopes, the kind made of delicate white paper, the kind that looks as if it will easily tear.

I think about the mothers waiting for them, the black-haired women I imagine in rustic rooms, rooms covered with intricate carpets, carpets full of woven flowers, flowers bursting next to bouquets of vegetables, beasts, and birds. I imagine the country itself with its thick forests, its swamps, its rice paddies, its wildflowers carpeting stony hills. I imagine the trees of Iran, the poplars, the myrtle, the kunars. And always my mind returns to the mothers, the women I imagine weeping secretly into colorful scarves, the women cooking dinners of okra stew and rice and lentils and lima beans and missing these boys who will always be boys to them, these boys that tonight I see as men.

We all sit down to dinner, a meal of chicken and rice made with a whole world of spices I cannot begin to name. We make small talk, asking one another the names of our hometowns, the numbers of brothers and sisters we have, whether or not our families have cats. We speak of Japan, what we like about living here, how the food is so delicious, the people so kind.

And after dinner, Amir's friends tell me they hope I will visit again some time and I am flattered and say that I hope I can and for a split second, I think such a visit might come to be. The whole night feels blessed, as if a thread of fine saffron were running through our words, creating a perfect golden line.

Then Amir emerges from the kitchen carrying a tray of hot tea and plate of sugar. We sit at the low table once more, kneeling Japanese-style. Amir gestures for me to put a cube of sugar on my tongue before drinking the tea, as is the custom in the country where he comes from.

The tea melts the sugar instantly in one delicious rush so that years later, when I remember to keep him near, this is how I think of Amir: a sweet, fleeting, perfect dissolve.

ne afternoon, all the men in my country are all busy or away and I am free for the afternoon of my ABC School responsibilities. So I hop a train and go downtown. Downtown is pale and deserted and still — empty of schoolchildren who are still in school, empty of grown-ups who are all at work.

Downtown-san, how very Zen you are today, I say, but Downtown-san is so Zen, it just looks back, cool and detached, a soul of stone gray.

I wander around the shops in the train station, looking at the plastic food in restaurant windows, the plastic facsimiles so common here. They do not look real. That's what makes them so compelling: that no one tries to pretend the plastic food is real. Then I duck into Midori, a large department store, where I find a pair of brown sandals that cost 10,000 yen or the equivalent of $70, which is twice as much as I am accustomed to paying for shoes and more than I can legitimately afford. Still, I buy them, and buying them feels good, a calm purchase of something that I know should belong to me.

Next I go to a bookstore and buy a Japanese magazine and then I settle myself into a booth where I order chocolate cake and coffee and I eat and drink and feel generally pleased with myself, with the cake, with the coffee, with the thought of wearing these new sandals, which, on top of looking good also smell fine in the way only decent leather can. I thumb through my magazine without worrying about words I cannot read. Instead, I enjoy the pictures, including one I stare at for a long time, then tear out to save: a black-and-white photograph of a glass bottle in swirls and shades of gray, something subtle and theatrical going on all at once.

A picture borne of solidity from a liquid rush.

I remember a couple standing in a small kitchen, making dinner one night. The season is summer. The air is thick. The man is Nozaki. The woman is me. What happens next I can see in a series of snapshots, *click, click, click.*

After the lull, the fall begins. Not all at once but gradually.

He cuts tomatoes. She watches the pasta cook. She has gone to a great deal of trouble to hunt down a jar of artichoke hearts and hopes he will like them, this delicacy he has never tried.

But after one bite, he makes a face.

Too sour, he says, and she eats the hearts alone that night.

They take the length of his futons one night to watch *The Big Blue,* a French film based on a real-life diver who, compelled to keep going deeper and deeper, gives up everything, including the woman he loves, so he can swim with the dolphins, eventually diving to his death.

What are your dolphins? she asks when the film is through. *What is it that compels you?*

I don't know, he says, mouth yawning, body folding, eyes closing.

They go to an arts and crafts fair and walk around, looking but not touching all the dishes on display. Such perfect dishes—slick platters in blue and white; fine white bowls with crazy black calligraphy swirls; tumblers made of rough red clay, the imprint of the artist's hands exposed.

She wants to buy these tumblers that seem so philosophically complex, so curious, such a contradiction in terms: *glasses* made of *clay.* She has seen such a thing before but never like this and she likes the way the red clay contrasts with the smooth pale green surface inside the tumblers, a splash of green that spills over the lip of the rim, the rim where the mouth could comfortably live.

She wants them but here he is beside her and she is too embarrassed to say: *Here is something I desperately want. Here is something I cannot live without.* She is a woman who should be traveling light in the world, after all, staying as she is in this country now, so temporarily. She does not need more dishes. She does not need anything more at all. Her desires would only be an embarrassment, she thinks, to the man who now walks several paces ahead.

Did you see anything interesting? he asks as they are leaving the park, heading back to his car.

Nothing, she says, looking up toward the sky. She pretends to be breezy, to be happy, to be content with him, walking from this crafts fair, headed back now to the car. She wants for nothing, she says.

A woman and a man at a Mexican restaurant. Pretty young waitress. A table, sangria, a basket of tortilla chips. I remember the headache from that sangria. A wall with a five-foot-tall Bart Simpson painted on. Bart's wearing a colorful Mexican hat. Bart's saying in Japanese, *Mexican food is delicious, dude!*

Ahead of them the whole afternoon.

The man looks tired.

The woman remembers the students who say *I am boring* for *I am bored* or *I am exciting* for *I am excited.*

I am boring today, she thinks. Nozaki is too. She fears he is also deeply bored as well.

What is your perfect vacation? she asks. The sangria reminds her that there is a whole world beyond Japan out there, all kinds of places where people know how to play. She's not a woman given to playing. She's too awkward in her body to let loose without thinking. But sometimes she plays. Once she went to Thailand, to Ko Samui and met a young Dutch man who de-boned her fish. Dinner led to walking. Walking to the ocean. At the ocean, clothes fell like dusk.

They used to talk about traveling. He used to want to know what she thought of Japan, what she really thought, deep down. She used to tell him things. She told him once about a trip to Sado Island she took her first year here, how Sado Island was the most beautiful place in Japan she had seen, relaxed in a way so different from most Japanese cities, completely Japanese and apart somehow. She was already imagining what it would be like to visit Sado Island with Nozaki soon. What it would be like to dance with him as Kodō, the Japanese drummers, played. Maybe it would have rained the night before. Maybe they would sink into the music together, dancing and sinking in mud, that mixture of earth and ocean, of solidity and fluidity. Everything at once: to be standing and sinking under the sky.

Nozaki asked her once where home was for her and she said Utah, Salt Lake City. *You know where I'm from!* The mountains, the desert. A place where contradictions are carved into the landscape, red rocks to the south, green forests to the north. *But you already knew that, right?*

But where, he asks, *are your—*

He stopped to look a word up in the dictionaries. They had stretched themselves out on the futons in the living room, the dictionaries between them. Back then they opened the tissue-thin pages of the dictionaries frequently and with ease, which gave their conversations a slow, ritualized quality, as if each word meant something fuller than it did before, as if each word were scripture.

Where are your sympathies?

And she realized he was asking about the geography of the heart.

The perfect vacation? he says. He's rubbing his head.

His sympathies, he said that night on the futons, were not with America or Europe or Japan but Brazil and hers leaned toward the Czech Republic. They talked that night about how strange it is, how you can feel kinship to a place even though you've never been, the idea of the place becoming as real as anything. They used to talk as if anything were possible. As if they might go to Sado Island together. Or Rio. Or Prague. They used to touch.

The sangria, she thinks, is going to her head. *The perfect vacation?*

To sleep, Nozaki says. *My perfect vacation is to sleep.*

One night he is supposed to call at 6 P.M., which he does, but she doesn't get the message until an hour later when she is immersed in a class at the ABC School, filling in for a teacher who failed to show.

When she calls him at seven, there's no answer at his place. So she calls again at eight, then at nine, and again at ten. Finally, before midnight, he answers his phone, sounding angry and maybe a little drunk.

So you don't want to get together? the woman asks, disappointed that he's not as eager to see her as she is to see him. All she wanted that night was to hear his voice. Now that she has his voice, his voice in her ear, it isn't enough. Whatever she has, she will always want more. The stakes go up. This her way of life. Her way of love. She wants to see him, even if it's only for a few minutes, just to say goodnight. And if she sees him? She will want to touch him. And then?

I want to sleep, he says.

I do too but not as much as I want to see you.

She is surprised that things have begun to go so stunningly wrong.

To pinpoint when the wrongness began is like trying to find a needle in a haystack, like trying to find one Japanese man in a crowd of men in Japan.

Call me tomorrow, she says.

And when he doesn't? She ducks out of the ABC School to go back to the arts and crafts show where she buys two clay glasses, only to walk away, then, minutes later, return as dusk presses in to buy six more.

remember this: A group of girls rescuing kittens abandoned in the forest on the outskirts of school. The girls kept the kittens in the English teachers' small, crowded room. Between classes, they ran to the box where the kittens huddled, cooing out loud, holding each kitten up. The kittens wriggled when held, made tiny sounds from perfect pink and o-shaped mouths.

Tiny as teacups.

I pointed to them one by one. *Small, smaller, smallest,* I said.

Kawaii, kawaii. So cute, each fragile *neko-chan.*

The next morning, the kittens were dead, their small bodies limp and still. The girls picked them up again, one by one, bending dead-kitten arms like Gumby dolls.

Kawaisō, they say. *Kawaisō.* Such a pity. Such a shame.

Didn't anyone FEED the cats last night? I hissed.

Mr. Mura, the head English teacher, shrugged.

Shō ga nai. It can't be helped.

The girls raced to class, then returned to the teachers' room afterward to stroke the dead kittens' stiffening fur.

Kawaisō, they cried, their voices falling, melodic, flute-like.

Small deaths. Like travel. As natural as a waterfall.

meet the professor for coffee, Amir for *ramen*. I ask each one separately to go see the *The Age of Innocence*, thinking only one of the two will come through, anyway.

Inside the dark theater, I hold the professor's hand, conscious of how he's watching, utterly rapt as imploded lives unfold on the screen and Newland Archer unbuttons Ellen Olenska's glove and Newland Archer says he has missed out on the flower of life. And when the film ends, I let go of the professor's hand and I remember hearing a famous French writer's definition of tragedy: the poorly timed.

With Amir *The Age of Innocence* is a mistake from the start: a movie subtitled in Japanese words he cannot read, the spoken English too fast for him to understand. Plus, the film's ornate setting and slow moving plot is dull beyond belief to Amir. I should have suggested an action flick — something other than a period piece, something that would be easy to watch, something that moved fast and didn't rely on so much verbal nuance.

Let's go, I say, after watching Amir squirm for half an hour in his seat.

Outside the theater, Amir opens his arms wide like he's just been released.

Omoshiroi? I ask, teasing him.

NO, he says. *Not at all. NOTHING about that was interesting!*

We walk around town afterward, afternoon turning to dusk, and Amir holds my hand and tells me I'm pretty and sings me songs in a minor key. The songs could be childhood lullabies or jingles for soapsuds from Iranian TV. All I know is that they sound like gifts from the gods through this man to me.

I tell Nozaki we have to go see *The Age of Innocence*, that he will absolutely love this film. But our timing's off, the film is gone, and we agree to see a Hollywood legal thriller instead.

We plan to meet at the theater, one of my favorite places in town — an old theater with a huge screen and wooden seats and a sticky unceremonial concrete floor. But when I arrive outside the theater there are all these men waiting in line and they all have the same dark hair and they all look to be between youth and middle age and I stand there staring and looking for Nozaki becomes painful, all these Japanese men blurring together, becoming part of some monolithic and maddening whole like those children's books with look-alike boys. Where's Waldo? Where's Nozaki?

I start to panic, to imagine Nozaki has crashed his car, that he is dead now and who will tell me? Who am I to tell? Finally Nozaki appears, looking tired, dark circles under his eyes. He touches my arm and a shiver runs through me. Relief. He is alive.

I couldn't see you, I say.

Sorry, he says. *I had a client that took some time.*

I want to tell him, *I thought you'd died. I almost started to cry.*

But we're late for the movie now and the theater is packed, so we rush in and find two seats and within minutes, the thriller takes over and Nozaki falls asleep and I close my eyes, trying to remember the last time he touched me, trying to remember the last time we touched. This man might as well be dead, this man will always be asleep. To me, he is always just beyond reach.

Is this when it started? Is this when things began to go wrong?

I could go back further. History compels.

What do you want from me? I asked Nozaki one evening in a bar. *I mean really, what do you want?*

I was not trying to script this. I wanted to know. *Because clearly there's something I'm missing here.*

Everything and nothing, he said.

An answer that could mean anything, a blow-off or a beautiful haiku.

I wonder what I want from Nozaki, too. For him to move with me to the United States while I study and write? I can't see him changing apartments, let alone moving across an ocean to start a new life. He's nearly forty years old, has a profession, and a cat. His sister lives down the street from him. Do I want for him to give that up? Work as a waiter in a sushi restaurant in Iowa? Take free English classes at the Presbyterian church at night?

Or would I be willing to stay here in this small town? My mind reels with images of what the future might be. How I might be. Forever resisting or unable to master proper Japanese? I see myself raising a child to whom I can ask only the simplest of things. *Do you like apples? Do you like persimmon?* And if the child did not respond back in text-book fashion? *Yes, I do. No, I don't.* Would we hire a fulltime interpreter to live with us?

In my mind, the future, which I want as a refuge, as home, collapses under the weight of simple phrases in my head. *Do you like apples? Yes, I do. Do you like persimmon? No, I don't. Do you like apples? Yes, I do. Do you like persimmon? No, I don't.*

Nozaki calls one night and says we need to talk. He picks me up. We go to a bar.

He knows, he says, he has not told me enough.

I wait for more and finally he says, *Ours is a layered relationship.*

The waitress arrives with two beers and yakitori in tow.

Itadakimasu.

Layered how? I ask.

A layered friendship, Nozaki says.

But is it only a friendship to Nozaki?

No, he answers, *this is not only a friendship.*

He is *conscious* of me as a woman.

We sit quietly. The yakitori turns cold.

I am conscious of him as a man.

Another bar, another night. Each one the same. Beautiful hostesses and tacky velvet booths and a glittering ball at the center of the room, silver and staged and twirling around and around and around. A drinker's moon.

Do you think I'm a cold man? he asks me.

His question surprises me.

Because if you do, he says, *that means it's as good as true.*

No, I say. *I don't. Not cold exactly. Just not here.*

I know, he says, *that I am pushing you away.*

It is his style to do this, he says, to pull away right when things with a woman begin to go well. It has happened before, he says. *My sister, old girlfriends — they all say I am a strange and difficult man.*

You are, I say. *And wonderful, too.*

He smiles and seems surprised by this last part and that, in turn, surprises me.

I try to look at him objectively and when I do, I am astonished at what I see: a version of my father's body, a man slight of build, a man with thin legs now crossed like a girl's, a man whose soft upper arms seem to lack muscular strength.

Is this what draws me to him? Some desire to find the father.

Here are two men always shrouded in smoke.

Here are two men always out of my reach.

Here is a pattern we both know well. This push and this pull between a man and woman, this dull and unfortunate international script. I'm struck now by how history weighs on us, how predictable our story seems. I know how this evening will end, how this story will end, how we will both go home alone tonight, how we will soon be separated by an ocean and numerous nation-states, how this no-win, push-pull, tug-of-war game will leave us suffering from scrapes of rope burn, that will leave us both fallen, covered in shit.

His feelings for me are strong, he says. *That part hasn't changed at all.* Then, *I love you, but . . .*

But what? I ask Nozaki, shrugging, having resigned myself to hearing the truth, having prepared myself now for listening to him list qualifiers like beads on a string. There is almost something comforting in this, in the familiarity of hearing a man in a foreign country saying the same things the men at home always did. And I have told Nozaki all about this before, how the men in my past have always said they loved me and I believe each one did, but the words always came with a qualifier — I love you *but* —

But? I say. I smile. I might as well help him along.

But nothing, he says. *I love you . . . and nothing.*

And later this will seem to me the terrible truth. That he loves me. That nothing will follow from that.

remember Nozaki in snapshots now: Nozaki in faded Levi's, an old sweatshirt. His hair greasy. I'm thinking he looks handsome this night, that it's just this greasy hair that men before have lacked.

He has had car trouble earlier. Changed a tire all by himself. Never got a chance to go to the baths. He goes to the *sentō*; his apartment does not have a bath. And now, tonight, the laces on his running shoes are coming undone and his hair is greasy and we're out and I'm so happy to be with him, to be out and on our way to a restaurant, and when he comes around the corner of the car, after he's parked, he starts to trip, then catches himself.

Are you OK? I ask, then in a split second see he's embarrassed I saw him, not hurt.

So here is the man I love in two parts: adorably messed up and boyish, about to trip over his own two clumsy feet; and a man deeply ashamed to make a small mistake.

One night, driving in his car, I think of what I know of him. That he lived in Tokyo for ten years before returning here. That he and his sister cared for their dying father. That he and his sister get along well. That his mother died many years ago.

So you're an orphan now, I tell him. The thought of him parentless and childless makes me sad, as if he were wedded to world of loss.

No, he says, as if scolding me. *An orphan is a child.*

Once, on a Sunday afternoon, he comes to pick me up at the ABC School. I have fallen asleep on the pink couch and when he comes in, I wake up, horrified that he has seen me, mid-day, asleep.

Years later, I continue to dream about him. Here's one from not so long ago: We are sleeping on a large wrought-iron bed. The bed sits center stage in a large, empty room, the kind with hardwood floors and high ceilings and elegant, old-fashioned moldings out of another century, some time other than now.

In the dream room there are no furnishings at all, no chintz couches or polished armoires, no fluffy chairs, no small black couch. It is large and largely empty, monastic in an aesthetically pleasing way, with nothing but the bed in the middle, positioned like a single vase of flowers in the alcove of a Japanese hall. Spare and lean. Also, the kind of contradiction I love: complete and full.

In the dream room, we wake from under plain white cotton sheets. His cleaning lady raps on the door, then quietly lets herself in. She gasps in horror and I understand that the source is the sight of me, a woman, a *foreign* woman right here in plain sight *and in bed.*

I pull the sheets to cover myself and listen as he defends me in language I recognize but fail to comprehend. The words are mysterious but the point perfectly clear: she stays, he says, and you can go, he tells the lady, and with that the cleaning lady — poof! — disappears.

What happens next is what interests me most. He farts — one small, delicate pop — and we laugh and then curl back up in that big, beautiful white bed. Or is it me in the dream who farts?

I cannot remember now. All I know is that when I wake, I realize the surprise is a surprise. It isn't his loyalty that touches me now but the ease with which we respond to that small bodily sound. In waking hours all those many years ago, we were too embarrassed by our bodies to ever *laugh.* And I remember how it was, in what ways we were the same: how we built fragile houses made of words; how we lived our real lives in our heads; how our bodies, sadly, caught us off guard.

He drives me home, holding a cigarette in one hand, turning the radio with the other. Shadows of pine trees flicker by outside. I can pick out a word here, a phrase there, but my Japanese is too sketchy to make sense of something as complicated as the radio's nightly news.

I wonder if this is as good it gets. The news as static, the man nearby.

In my bag are dictionaries. At home I have folded the corners of pages as if beginning a series of *origami* swans, as if what I say to Nozaki will make all the difference.

Serious. Shimmer. Significant. Situation.

I have studied these words, marking ones we might use.

Kōsaku suru. Yamuoezu. To cultivate. Compelling.

I have attempted to memorize the Japanese words.

Kore kara. From now on.

Kore-kara-no. The future.

Kore made. Up to this time.

But here in his car, my memory fails and it is too dark to see.

He rolls down the window, throws his cigarette out.

I stretch my head out the window to see if I can see the moon. All I want is fresh air and a look at the moon, whether it's full or slender, yellow or white.

Nozaki looks over at me like I'm a child. Maybe he's thinking I want to jump.

Marilyn-san, he says, motioning to pull me back.

It's OK, I say, settling back into my seat, rolling the window up.

Anyway, I can't see the moon, I say, looking toward the man inside the car, shadows fluttering across his face.

I stop sleeping at Sara's and move back to spending nights solely in Natsume-san's spare room, a large room empty of all but thick luxurious futons and fresh new *tatami* mats — a space I would enjoy if I were able to sleep in the room. My logic is simple: If I stay at Natsume-san's, I can stay later at the ABC School at night. If I stay in Shiojiri, I will be closer to him. And if I learn Japanese? My desire to learn Japanese quickens and flares and lists continue lining notebook after notebook, words start piling up, as if the words I learn and what I say to Nozaki will turn things around, will turn everything around, as if what I say could make such a difference, as if the words themselves, untethered from speech and exiled from the nest a sentence can make, will make all the difference. As if.

Mono-no-wakatta. Sensible.

Kannō-teki-na. Sensual.

Riko-teki-na. Jibun-hon-i-no. Selfish.

These lists are my animal sounds.

Is it selfish to want someone? the hand writes, as if the hand has a mind of its own. The hand attached to the body curled up, the body on the ABC School's pink couch. The ears can hear the cash register ringing in the liquor store below, salarymen outside living it up. It is late now. The school closed hours ago. The eyes see red tulips in a vase, flashcards neatly stored away, portraits of black-eyed children lining the wall. And stars, so many stars, and questions, so many questions, all the questions on the wall printed in sturdy black ink. She wonders.

Is it selfish to want to make someone your dream?

And this is the season that I study on the couch every night and then slink out to Natsume-san's house behind the school, sleeping fitfully in those perfect futons, waking to the sound of glass breaking. Outside the window, an old man from the liquor store dumps whole crates of beer bottles onto the ground and I wake up to the sound of glass breaking and for a moment, before I am fully awake, I think something terrible has happened, that there has been an accident, that maybe someone had died.

But there never is an accident. Just an ordinary routine. A series of gestures. A turn of the shoulder. A twist of the hips. A crate lifted, then dropped. Silence, then a crash. An old man who knows they're easier to move, these small pieces of broken glass. An old man who understands the necessity of making a mess.

Then it happens. We meet for a drink. We talk. Nothing feels started or ended, nothing feels alive or resolved. Nozaki drives me home, drops me off in front of the ABC School and Natsume-san's house. There is nothing unusual about this night, save one small gesture. The absence of a gesture.

Goodnight, he says.

Goodnight, she says, moving to kiss him on the cheek.

And the man turns away.

And not right then, but later, the mind catches up with what the body takes in, what the body right now would like desperately to ignore.

And it's over, the body knows. *It's through. This man is through with you.*

know a woman who spent some time in the loony bin. That's what she called it, *the loony bin*. Her fiancée had put a shotgun to his head after a long struggle with cocaine and booze and that sent this woman right around the bend. She told me about her stay in the loony bin, which lasted two weeks, without any embarrassment.

But there were other things, she said. Things she had done leading up to the loony bin. Things she didn't like to talk about.

Like what? I asked.

Well, she said. Really, she was too embarrassed to say.

I tried to imagine the worst but the worst didn't seem that bad and then my mind stalled.

I licked an ashtray, she finally said. When her fiancée died, she could not bear to throw away the remnants of a full ashtray from his house. And one night, in the midst of hearing voices, she licked it, consuming the ashes of his old cigarettes, taking the ashes in with the tenderness of a kiss.

You were sick with grief, I said, *understandably out of your head.*

The woman smiled. Her eyes were half moons that disappeared when she laughed.

I wanted to tell her about living in Japan and the man who turned away from me but it seemed kind of small, even next to an ashtray. So I sat there, quiet and sad, wishing I had something, even two weeks in the loony bin, to prove where I'd been, something to show her I knew the right questions if not the right answers, that I understood as I understand now. Weren't we all crazy once? Stricken with some wild, unruly grief?

Expatriate friends, people who have already left Japan, write letters that arrive at the ABC School, telling me to be sure to travel through

Asia before returning home. *Don't miss the chance.* One says the food in Vietnam is unbelievable, some five hundred national dishes. Indonesia, another writes, is by far the most interesting place he has ever seen. *Don't miss it,* he warns as if anticipating what he knows I am doing, have done: missing that chance to take another one.

When are you coming? another writes to ask. She lives in Thailand and wants me to make good on a promise made months before to book a flight to Chiang Mai in June so we can go trekking together in the north. All the guidebooks recommend trekking in the north. *You'll love it,* she writes. I put off writing back and later she tells me she knew something important was up, that I was either unhappy or in love, or maybe — probably — both.

Later she would fill me in on the complications of her own life at that time, the darkness beyond what she allowed herself, in cheerful letters, to write. Her story, too, involved a certain foreign man. Someone obsessive about her, someone who scared and thrilled her and held her, for many months, mentally captive in a place she didn't belong. Those are the words she would use later: *mentally captive in a place I didn't belong.* But at the time, she was lulled into thinking it was all so normal, just part of the seduction of a new country. And she acted the role of ambassador of goodwill, writing letters that read like eloquent travel brochures. *You won't believe the flowers here — the orchids, the bougainvillea. I promise you, you'll want to stay forever.*

Stay forever.

Yes, that's what I want to do. Stay forever but not in the orchids, not in bougainvillea. Here in Japan. Here in a place famous for its *soba,* here in a place famous for sweet wine.

Here is where the wine is.

Here is where the men are.

Here is where I am.

I am, I am, I am.

One night I go to the Ito-yokado coffee shop to meet Amir. On the way, I run into two women, American English teachers like me. They ask when I am leaving. I tell them I'm not sure and ask, *How about you?*

They are planning to leave in just a few more weeks when their teaching contracts run out. Then they will travel in Asia, just as I had planned, as we all planned — to travel the world and become broadminded before settling down and returning home.

Home.

I met a biologist once who studied the neurology of birds. Certain species are genetically coded to hear a song, he said. Remove that part of their brain and you effectively remove their ability to go home.

Home.

I read somewhere that Henry David Thoreau left Walden on weekends so his mother could cook and do his laundry for him.

Home.

Anyone with half a brain, I told the biologist, *wouldn't want to go home looking like that.*

The bus station is empty, the shops all closed and I am sorry because I had wanted to buy some lilies tonight but I can't because it's already too late and anyway, I don't have a home anymore, don't have a table on which I can put the lilies tonight. "Moon River" plays on the speakers and I think about how a few years ago that song, my mother's favorite, would have affected me, would have sent me back into a reverie, thinking about my mother and the lines on my beautiful mother's face. Now the song is nearly over before I even notice it, the song that seems vaguely familiar and completely ordinary, something easily forgettable, certainly nothing to stir homesickness or nostalgia or anything else.

It's just a song. Nothing more.

And I wonder, is this what will happen if I find a way to stay? All the old memories will get crowded out? All the old touchstones will get replaced? It used to be that one whiff of smoke reminded me only of my father. Now it's Nozaki's face I see in the haze. It used to be I thought of my mother all the time. Now I forget I have one, she's so far away.

This could happen anywhere, of course. Maybe this *would* happen anywhere, this pulling away, this snap of one life in favor of something else, this replacement theory, this crowding out.

But if I stay here, it will happen here. Is this where I want all that forgetting to take place?

One of the women breaks the spell, asks me again, *So when do you leave?* and I think, *I don't know, I wish I knew, but the thing is, I don't really want to stay and I don't exactly want to go.*

Who knows, I say. *Sometimes I think I'd like to just stay put.*

So what will you do? she asks, and I realize she means long-term, *after* Japan, as if it's a done deal, as if it would be crazy to stay here indefinitely. I remember meeting an Australian man at a party once who said he didn't understand the impulse toward the expatriate life. *How can you live indefinitely*, he wondered, *in a place that doesn't allow you to vote?*

I listened to him and understood that rationally, of course, he was exactly right, that citizenship made a difference, that it was a little crazy to live on the fringes of a place year after year, no fluency quite in sight, that something in that wasn't quite right.

But I also knew that for me, the connection to country, the connection to place, it would never be rational, would always be this: an allegiance to something sensual, something absurd but concrete, to the taste of persimmon, to the smell of *obon* fires at night, to the possibility of seeing a certain man step into morning light.

To the question, *What color is the sun?*

To the answer the children at the ABC School always give.

The sun is red, Miss Marilyn.

And to the men.

Go back to school, go to graduate school, I tell the women at the station, remembering my mother's philosophy that you can never have too much education or too many dishes in your life and wondering if it's true, that no one ever regretted going to graduate school. I wonder how I will survive graduate school when right now my brain is far too tired to learn. I wonder if these women can tell that the prospect of graduate school means nothing to me, that the thought of leaving here holds no appeal.

I try to guess how old these women are and figure they are maybe in their mid-twenties somewhere. I try to imagine what their experiences have been, if they have fallen in love with the particulars of this country yet, if they have fallen in love with a particular someone. What I want to know is if they are as mixed up as I am but I am too mixed up to begin to guess.

Are you sorry to go? I ask.

Kind of, one woman says.

In a way, chimes the other. *But it's time, you know what I mean? You can't stay forever. I mean this isn't real life.*

I nod in agreement, though it's a phrase I've never fully understood. What's unreal about the three of us standing here now?

Then I blurt out that I have just met someone, a guy, someone I really like, and *it's kind of complicated, you know?* I leave out the complications, that it's not one man but three. I leave out that the one who matters has drifted away. I leave out, too, the continuing refrain. *I'm not sure I want to go. I'm not sure I want to stay.* I'm having trouble concentrating. I'm having trouble going through the motions required of the smallest social exchange.

Yeah, isn't it always when you're leaving that you meet someone, one says. She speaks as if the tragedy of poor timing were a natural thing.

Then we all laugh even though I don't feel much like laughing, and the other woman says, as if the truth bears repeating, *Doesn't it always work out that way,* only the way she says it, it isn't a question.

And they leave and "Moon River" ends and I am standing there alone, still waiting for Amir, wondering. *Does it? Does it?*

emembering is a way to keep someone near. I have remembered now for seven years. And what I try to remember isn't just the men or the country but also the woman who was me. The me who bought an expensive bottle of champagne one day. Then brought that bottle to a certain man's place one day at noon. The me who believed that love was worth celebrating, troubled and troubling as that love may be.

I have a meeting, the man said, promising to be back by 1 o'clock.

At two the woman went shopping. Sat down in a cafe to drink a cup of café au lait. Read a magazine, borrowed from an expatriate friend, a magazine filled with words about a famous poet who wrote and wrote and wrote and wrote and then stuck her head in the oven and fell asleep.

Later, her husband married the woman he'd been having an affair with and *that* woman went and put *her* head in the oven too, as if this head-in-the-oven business were a very cruel but inescapable little copycat trick.

Or maybe there was something wrong with the oven. A pilot light that kept going out.

At three the woman goes for a walk.

At four she decides it is time to celebrate.

She returns to his house. Pops open a bottle of champagne. Watches the cork fly high, hitting the ceiling and leaving, she suspects, a mark she can now do nothing about. Will he notice? she wonders. Will he care? All celebrations leave their mark, all travel leaves its trace. She wishes she had bought more bottles of more champagne and she would open every one, hitting and leaving her mark.

She drinks and drinks and drinks and drinks, one glorious solitary swig after another, and isn't it interesting, she thinks, that it has taken her so long to discover the pleasure of what that word, *swig,* means?

She decides this is a party and she wants to dance. He isn't home so she dances anyway, waltzing around his kitchen, moving to the sound of the words in her head, gliding on his dirty hardwood floors, giddy from the sparkling champagne, singing to herself, *You have a pencil in your ear, a pencil in your ear. Excuse me, Miss, what's that? That? Oh, nothing. I have a pencil in my ear.*

She gets toasted.

Toasted.

She remembers a night early on, when she'd just arrived in this country. Her neighbors had given her a welcome-to-the-country party.

Food. Champagne. A large bouquet of flowers as if she were a princess, *a goddamned princess, I tell you,* she told Ellen when Ellen called that night from the United States. One of the neighbors, a young handsome man, taught her slowly the names of body parts. Eyes. *Me.* Nose. *Hana.* Mouth. *Kuchi.* Shoulders. *Kata.* She tried to teach him how to raise a glass of champagne to make a toast. But the word — *toast* — went over his head.

Bread? he said. Yes, he liked bread.

She was too toasted at the time to sort things out.

And now here she is, several years later, toasted again.

Toasted.

Her whole body is toasted and aches.

Her whole head is filled with junk.

Clichés she knows are not quite right. As sorry as a sandwich? As quiet as a rat?

She remembers an article from a small-town newspaper long ago. A 78-year-old woman killed her husband. *Why?* the judge asked. So late in the game. *Because he ate my chocolate Easter bunny,* she said.

She arches her back to get the kinks out, notes she is a cat in heat, eager and urgent and out of control. She takes from her black bag a bottle of perfume. She sprays the perfume into the air, onto his books, into the dull white sheets of his low, narrow bed, indiscriminately spraying, marking this territory, claiming it as her own. She thinks of herself as male and female now, aggressively and prettily able to piss perfume. Perfume all over these stark white walls. Perfume she hopes will leave a stain.

She repeats his words now.

Love is wide. Love is wide.

Love is a wide-assed woman, naked on the bed. A woman covered in gruel, throwing crockery in the kitchen. A woman screaming from the bedroom to be fed, fucked and wed. Love is a wide-mouthed infant, a black hole of need. Love squats and shits inside the head. Love is dread.

Click, click, click.

She makes a mental list of all that wide love is or can be, its fierce family of hierarchies, of needs. She makes a mental note of what she sees, hoping, now that she has started her little party tonight, that he won't come home at all.

Stacks of comic books up against a wall. The kitchen table covered with empty whisky bottles. The faint smell of urine but no sign of the cat. The cat's name sounds like a fur ball. *Kaki? Kaki?*

The *manga* reminds her. There have been other men.

The professor, for instance.

Once, she asked the professor if he would be willing to do some translations for her—translations of Japanese children's books; translations of *manga* she had been wondering about.

He agreed too easily.

Are you sure? she said. She felt she was taking advantage of him. *You know, don't you, that I'd be happy to pay?*

Don't be ridiculous, the professor said. *I'm glad for the chance to be practicing my English. I would do anything for the chance to talk with you.*

And so, they met one Saturday morning in their Adultery Coffee Shop after the professor had done the homework she had assigned.

This one, he said, *is a typical Japanese story that has typically Japanese sexist expressions in it.*

What do you mean?

That girls are kind. That boys should be brave.

The story was about a ten-year-old girl who met up with a witch and the witch was the mountain personified. The witch-mountain asked the girl, did she know why there were so many flowers blooming there? The girl said no. The mountain told the girl that each time someone did something good—when a man was brave and sacrificed himself; when a young girl was kind and gave up her desire for her sister's sake—a new flower bloomed.

So the emphasis, the professor said, as he finished the translation, page by page, *is very Japanese. All about endurance. The importance of endurance.*

The *manga* were next, the comic books she had seen the men lined up at 7-Eleven to read. She thought the *manga* were pornographic and racist as well, relying as they did on provocative images of *gaijin* women, all blonde and busty and primed for cat fights with Japanese women. She hated that.

Aren't they annoying, she told the professor. Even without being able to read a single word she knew what she knew. She had decided in advance.

But these women are not gaijin, the professor said, pointing to the Wonder Women types. *In the stories here, they are Japanese.*

Are you sure? she said.

Yes, the professor continued.

Well, what do the words say?

It's difficult to say.

The professor stumbled, said the comics relied too heavily on slang he didn't know well, then finally admitted he could not read these pornographic stories in this way, could not read them while sitting there in this coffee shop next to her.

It is a hell . . . it is a torture, he said, *to look at these pictures and to sit near you.*

Torture. Endurance.

Love is hell.

A wide word.

Baby, baby it's a wide world.

There's more. She sees more.

His coats lined up on open racks, a green neon ski jacket. She didn't know that he could ski. Books piled in stacks on the floor. Books she cannot read. And CDs. So many CDs. The CDs remind her of those boys she liked in high school, the tall, thin, quiet ones who were smart but never studied, who were handsome in an awkward, gangly way. They were outsiders, those boys, just a little rebellious, the ones who smoked pot and said *fuck* and listened to Todd Rundgren and Steve

Earle and Pink Floyd. She observes all this and she misses those boys, those sweet messed-up teenage boys.

Whatever happened to them?

What happened to her?

The bed, she observes. In the next room, a narrow bed — a squiggle, like the country on the map.

She moves toward it, the country of the bed. Sleeps the drunk man's dreamless and sobering sleep, which is to say, she sleeps like the dead.

Then she wakes to the sound of footsteps.

His.

He comes in. Sees the woman. Sees a plastic bag next to the woman, the bag in which she has, oh so delicately, if she does say so herself, thrown up, vomited, expelled all remnants of the party, rid her body of pleasure, rid her body of champagne.

She is nothing, if not observant. She takes in her surroundings even now.

The sound of the toilet flushing.

The man sitting on the edge of the bed.

The man asking, *Are you OK?*

No, she thinks. There are many ways to describe what she is now but one thing she is not is simply OK.

In a few weeks she will go to a movie at a theater in a city in the United States. The movie will be a love story about a middle-aged European woman living in the Midwest and a middle-aged American man who travels and takes pretty photographs. She will cry at the movie, knowing the movie is schmaltzy, that the critics will pan it, that the male lead, after all, is stiff as a board. But the story, a romance — this moves her. Romance remains so misunderstood. It's not about two people coming together. It's about alienation, then reunion with the self. The secret life of what we love.

When the movie ends, she will start to drive home and on the street at dusk she will pass a young woman in stocking feet and a small boy trailing close behind. She will slow down, shout out the window, ask the woman in stocking feet, *Are you OK?* and the woman, who will explain later that she just left a man who was beating the shit out of her, will stop in the middle of the street, answer, *Do I look OK?*

Do I look OK?

On the man's narrow squiggle of a bed the woman stretches out and remembers watching a man at Scotty's watch his girlfriend stumble out of the bar. The man went home and put a plastic bowl by his girlfriend's head and also a tall glass of water, just in case the woman woke up in the middle of the night, sick, which she did.

Is this love? To anticipate someone's weakness? To make allowances in advance?

She would like a tall glass of water right about now.

A tall glass of water. A sign of true love.

Nozaki sits next to her on the edge of his bed. He has turned on the television via remote control. There is a basketball game playing. She did not know he liked watching sports. She notes how boyish he looks, sitting there absorbed in an American basketball game. He puts the remote control down on the dresser by the bed, then picks up an earring that she left on the nightstand earlier. He holds the earring up to the light, examining its small indentations carved in gold, an archaeologist who has just discovered relics. A sign of an ancient civilization of women? He stares.

She remembers how he told her the date of his birthday once, early on. The same date, she said, as her father's birthday. *Isn't it strange*, she said. *Isn't there something strange in that?*

Then once a year Marilyn-san will think of me, he'd said.

She'd nodded. Said nothing. *Then once a year I will have an excuse.*

Her father. Her mother. The original travelers. The committers of original sin. She remembers seeing them touch when they were away from home, stepping out of a taxi in New Orleans, walking into a hotel in London, ducking out of the rain near a castle in Nagoya.

Later, when she sobers up and he has taken his place inside his small, monastic bed, she will sit beside him on that narrow bed and they will talk late into the night.

We are born alone and die alone, he says in Japanese.

Yes, dust to dust and ashes to ashes, she will say, suddenly given an understanding of phrases she shouldn't understand.

But in between? There's so much time, she says. *Just dance. Even if it isn't with me, promise me you'll dance.*

She pretends to do a little jig, wiggling her arms in the air, smiling big.

His eyes are cloudy, his body slack. He has always been asleep to her. This is their story: a fairy tale in which the prince never wakes up.

Wakatta? she asks. Her words rouse him.

Does he understand?

He stares. Shakes his head.

She wanders to the futon on the floor where she will fall asleep, then sneak out in the early morning light. She isn't sure if he means no, he won't, or no, he doesn't understand, and perhaps the difference doesn't matter tonight.

Remembering is the only way.

She remembers standing outside Nozaki's house, waiting for his curtains to move. Or, to be more precise, she remembers standing across the street from his house, watching his window, hoping his curtains will move.

He's probably out drinking at some hostess bar, getting wasted with the guys. Still, she waits. She is alive. To be alive is to be possessed. To be possessed is to know you cannot help yourself. She has dressed for the occasion, dressed to look like the foreigner she is. She's in lipstick, a skirt and too-tight shirt and a pair of black dressy shoes, the only ones she owns that have anything close to a heel. She has this idea that if she can just see him —

Fifteen minutes go by. Nothing. Another fifteen. Nothing more.

Someone approaches. She drops back into the shadows of an alley. This is a small town. As a blonde-haired *gaijin*, she stands out like a sore thumb, like a woman with a pencil in her ear.

She is lost and possessed and overdressed and she is hoping to see something, a glimpse, a shadow, a movement, a ripple of dark curtains moving in the night, curtains that, if they move, will tell her he's home and he's alive!

For this is the nature of her particular whirlpool of obsession this night: that because she hasn't seen him, she has now jumped to the fear that he is no longer alive, that he is lying there on his narrow bed, that he is, for reasons she cannot begin to comprehend, dead.

Dead.

It is the height of childishness: that if you can't see someone he must be dead. But there it is. She is sure he's dead and she wonders now what to do. Call the police? Bring Natsume-san to knock on his door?

She can remember waiting another five minutes, hoping for the curtains to rustle, to flicker, to come alive, to move. They don't. They never do.

Walking home, she passes one of those cemeteries where small stone statues wear red kerchiefs over smooth, stony heads and she tries to look for once, to see the expressions on the faces of these child monuments, these children of stone.

But it's too dark. The monuments to babies never born go unrecognized tonight. She cannot will herself to see in the dark. She cannot will those curtains to move. She cannot will the man to love a woman he does not love. Stone and cloth and people will do what stone and cloth and people must. And as she walks, her feet begin to hurt like the devil. This is your penance, she thinks, that these shoes are too tight, and she sings herself a little ditty, a little lullaby for the child within — *These shoes are made for stalking, and that's just what they'll do* — only the song doesn't seem funny, nothing is funny and a thought floats in and out of her head. *You'll never laugh about this.* And the funny thing is, that part will hold true.

When I tell the professor he has, of the three men, given me the least, I wonder what possesses me to say such awful things. He stares at his coffee, then off into space.

You're not in a position, I continue, hoping to soften this undeserved blow, *to give me what I need.* For this is the problem with married men: They're married.

I sigh in relief to see my words have had the desired effect, to see the professor turn his face back toward me, to see the light come back to his married and middle-aged face.

When I tell Amir I'm leaving soon, I repeat the verb *to leave* once in English, again in Japanese, but he shakes his head back and forth, refusing to hear. *No listen,* he says, *no listen,* and I am moved by this, a small act of denial, a refusal to face the truth.

I call my best friend, Ellen, again and again. Calling is my way of staying afloat. I call from lime green phone booths outside train stations and pale pink phone booths outside restaurants. I call again and again, always collect. *Helen-chan.* That's how the Japanese pronounced her name when she visited here. *Melon-chan.* Which is what she calls me.

Helen-chan listens as Melon-chan cries.

She can imagine the scene. The mix of *ramen* and incense from shops and Shinto shrines; the cars' exhausted fumes; the sound of trains. She went to a fortune teller on the streets of Matsumoto once on a visit here, a man who said to her *You will have trouble with your father.* Her father had been dead then for five years.

Ellen keeps saying the same thing again and again.

Just hold on. And get yourself on that plane.

And this, of course, is the simplest of acts but the one I can't imagine. Stepping onto a plane, walking down the ramp, moving through the rounded door — these actions now strike me as a sequence out of a terrible fairy tale, the plane some postmodern version of the gingerbread house, a place that will turn out to be a large oven, not a plane at all, a place where the flight attendants will serve me up in a *bentō* box for lunch.

I had a ticket. I had managed that much. All I had to do was get onto that plane, something I had done a hundred times before. But the mind apparently has a mind of its own. And mine rebelled against this inevitable act.

Yes, yes, I will, I say to Ellen's voice, dreamlike and unreal, separate from the person I used to know, the one with dark curly hair, pale skin, a small scar on her left cheek. I can't imagine her anymore. I can't imagine anything.

I have to leave. The writing is on the wall, I say. *I mean the calligraphy.*

That's good, that's good, Ellen says. *You're making a joke.*

Remembering is the only way.

We are sitting across from one another at a table in his law office so the conversation feels like a legal deal, something business-like, cold. The talk isn't languid, just painfully awkward and slow.

My feelings for Marilyn-san have not changed, he says, but if I deem his expressions of those feelings as changed then my perceptions make that as good as true.

Perceptions matter but perceptions are only translations, I say. *Feeling is the only thing with any integrity.*

Integrity?

I look it up in my dictionary and hand it to him.

Near perfect, he says, reading out loud.

Love is an act of will, I say. I do not know if I believe what I am saying or not. But these are the words coming out of my mouth.

Will? he says. *I do not know this word.*

I rifle through the dictionary again, push the definitions toward him. I remember a student at the ABC School who had copied her high school homework dutifully, writing one dozen times: *I do not know this work, I do not know this work, I do not know this work.*

The word is work. The dictionary's open.

Will. A noun suggesting conscious determination. *Will.* A grammatical construction of the future. *Will.* A sign of hope, of eagerness, of optimism, of faith.

After reading the definitions, he nods, says, *yes, that might be true, that love requires will. And maybe that is exactly what Nozaki lacks.*

In any case, he continues, *if Marilyn-san sees Nozaki as lacking will, the perception is as good as true.* If I think the evidence of his love is missing, it is as good as gone.

We continue talking.

Nozaki calls me *tokubetsu na* that night, only I mishear and think he's saying *separate.*

You want to separate?

He shakes his head.

Not separate. He flips through the dictionary, stopping to take long drags from his cigarette, and points to a word with *special* written as the translation to the side.

We spend a few more hours misunderstanding each other that night but finally, we are exhausted, we are done.

Are you relieved? I ask.

Nozaki leans back in his chair and closes his eyes and appears as if he might be ready to fall asleep. Later I read in a book targeted at Americans doing business with the Japanese that such a gesture means the person still has some thinking left to do.

Do not give up, the book's authors advised. *This does not mean the person with whom you are negotiating is bored.*

At the time, though, I translate the gesture as evidence Nozaki is angry or indifferent or maybe some combination of the two and because it is my perception, the thinking makes it true.

Are you relieved? I ask again, feeling a little angry, as if he *has* to answer, that if he does nothing else for me it will be to answer this question, provide a simple yes or no. I do not bother to ask him if he knows what *relieved* means.

No, not relieved, he says, opening his eyes, and something in the tone of his voice is so small and fragile and familiar that I understand. He is disappointed too.

Before leaving that night, I ask Nozaki for one last favor: to come with me to Tokyo in a few days to see me off at the airport.

I'm not asking if you can, I said. *I'm asking if you WILL.*

I will, he says, using the new vocabulary word cultivated from the night.

But Nozaki will not accompany me to the airport in Tokyo or anywhere else. Instead, he will hand me an umbrella the morning after the last night we spend together, one of those strange nights where, after the long haul of breaking up, we speak easily and naturally and even laugh a little.

We made curry and rice that night. I told him how, when I first came to Japan, I thought the packages for instant curry looked like insect repellent. And then we slept chastely side by side in his small narrow bed and in the morning, I slipped out early, before an ordinary day of work began for him, before my duties began at the ABC School.

In that in-between time before day began but after night was done, I walked back to Natsume-san's house, past the vineyards with their hats of crowny thorns, past the *pachinko* parlors, and past the building where I'd first met Nozaki among the Japanese businessmen.

Nozaki had stood by the window before I left and noticed that it was raining hard today and I could hear it, that rain, such loud rain, louder than any I'd heard before. To someone who grew up in a rainy country like Japan such loud, heavy rain may not be such a big deal but to me, someone born and raised in a desert, a very bony place, the rain was astounding, just astounding—no small thing.

Yes, I can hear, I said.

Then I gathered my things and headed for his door and in a gesture small and ordinary and final and sweet, he handed me an umbrella, a small blue cheap plastic umbrella, and he said *take care* as he watched me walk through the door and unlatch his blue gate.

And I never saw him again.

f it had ended there? With an exchange at his door about the weather that day? With the gift of an umbrella and a simple pair of good-byes? If it had ended on some note of dignity and calm?

In my remaining days I do not understand that it is over. The reality, as they say, is not sinking in.

The reality, my friend Rachel says, *is that it ain't over till some-body throws crockery.*

I continue working at the ABC School, but work—the teaching, the filing, the cutting up of construction paper moons and stars—provides no solace anymore.

Because I continue calling Nozaki.

Because he continues to will himself not to answer my calls.

I call him from work. I call him from home. When there's no answer, my body begins to rebel against itself as I embrace time-honored methods of distracting myself: drinking and eating and meeting with friends to excess—all in hopes of obliterating what has become a rush of feeling like a river, fast-running and deep.

My friends look at me funny when I say this is a river and I'm drowning here, can't you tell? For they are like anyone: they see no water, only a woman standing there on the sidewalk, in the bar, at the restaurant table, and she is talking, and everyone is talking, and we are all on solid, dry ground.

In my remaining days I go to Rose's house, Rose another expatriate in town, Rose who has pictures of a guru tacked up to her wall, Rose who talks while I listen. Or pretends to. For it is clear I am not absorbing much. The nature of a crack-up: the cracked are interested only in themselves.

What's going on? Rose asks.

It's this guy, I begin.

I tell her about only one of the men. Why muddy the waters? I reason. The waters are plenty dirty enough.

What it is about him? she asks.

I cringe at the question. *What do you mean?*

I mean, why do you like him so much?

I cringe again. This is all anyone wants to know of a love affair in the end. What was it about him? What was so special about her? As if *it* weren't *him*. As if *she*—a whole person—weren't enough. As if these things were rational, could be easily summed up.

Like him? I say. *Why?*

I mean, is it worth it? she asks. *This man, this pain?*

I stare at the pictures of the bearded guru staring from the walls. There are a thousand reasons not to fall in love and still we do it, we are stupid, predictable, we are a species that cannot help itself. We fall in love with teachers and countries and teapots and boys. This is not about a ledger of good or bad; this is not about whether the guy is worth it or not; this is just something I just have to get through now, to swim away, to save myself.

I should go, I tell Rose, declining her offer of another cup of tea. And then I do. I leave. I get onto my bike and go, go, go, riding my bike as fast as possible up toward Gofukuji temple, just so I can ride down the hill, riding past the rice fields and knowing this: that home is no longer a country or a house, that home is now limited to the inside of my crazy little head.

I meet Susan at a restaurant, Susan who is married to Kazuo, Susan who lives in an old house in the country, Susan who asks me to tell her everything and I try and afterward, it's clear that out of loyalty to me, she will see Nozaki as the fool.

He does not appreciate you, she says. *Love should not be so hard,* she says. *You should not have had to lure him with a carrot,* she says. *YOU are the carrot, darling! Go call him up and ask him to marry you!*

I leave the restaurant feeling momentarily better, tall and orange and desirable and thin, but within the hour, the feeling wears off and

I remember: Nozaki isn't a fool because he doesn't love me; he just doesn't love me. And I am a human bean, not a carrot, a human being still crazy about him.

In my remaining days, Shūko and Keiko take me with them to the baths one afternoon, where, in a room filled with steam, I watch as my friends wash themselves slowly and elegantly, cleaning themselves before entering the baths.

I admire my friends' fluidity and grace. I aspire to imitate their every move. How to fill a plastic washtub with a mixture of water, hot and cold; how to dip the washcloth; how to make the cloth lather up with soap; and how to clean the body slowly at first, and thoroughly, moving the cloth in circular motions, tenderly as if washing a baby, then rinsing, clean water down the back, over the breasts, between the legs, then filling the small tub with water again and pouring water over the head, through the hair, hair that is not, like everyone else's here, straight and shiny, as black as a lacquer box.

The *sentō* today is crowded, more so than any other time I've been. These women, old women with bellies gone slack, young women with breasts ripe as peaches — they vary in size and shape, but together they seem to blend, one into the next, the striking ones no longer distinguishable from the rest.

Keiko asks, *May I wash your back?*

Yes, I say, and she takes a cloth to the center of my back, moving it in circular motions, courteously avoiding the skin that leads to private parts. Afterward I do the same for her. And after that, Shūko and I take turns, too.

Later, when we've all submerged ourselves in the hot water of the bath, clean enough now that we can do just that, I close my eyes and wonder what it would be like to stay here, bathing at length as the day stretches from afternoon to evening, then from evening to night. I imagine waking here, lounging in the *sentō* for days. I imagine the languor of the setting, the comfort of the place, and I shudder to think of going back outside.

In reality, we would tire of the place should we stay too long, tire, too, of the leisurely pace. Our skin would shrivel up, our minds turn to mush. If we stayed at the baths, surely we would soon crave something else. Fresh air. Dry hair. The feel of clothes on our skin. We would miss elements of the outside world. The company of men, the complications their presence brings, the tension of their touch, which nothing else, for better or worse, can replicate.

When we leave the *sentō* that day I curl up in the back seat and Shūko asks, *Will Marilyn-sensei be OK?*

Yes, I will be OK. I feel momentarily whole. Luminous. Intact.

Shūko hugs me as I get out of the car, and Keiko does too, and our hair is still wet and we all smell good, and the light of the street lamp reminds me of a full moon and we stand there in a small circle, like schoolyard friends, holding hands about to wave goodbye but before we do, Shūko says *gambatte, gambatte,* to do my best, to endure. *This is an important time. Love will make Marilyn big.*

n my remaining days, I carry a plane ticket that indicates when I will be leaving this place, but the reality of leaving does not enter me. Three days before this ticket indicates I am to leave, I check myself into an anonymous hotel, the restlessness that defines me having reached a fever pitch.

Check-in time is 4 P.M. So I still have an hour to go. And there's no seat in the lobby of this small, clean hotel. The Tourist Hotel. Tourist. Of course. You are a tourist. Why did you think it could go another way?

Leave the hotel. Step into the sun. Find shade in a park. Sit under a tree. Forty-five minutes to go. Go get *ramen*, then. You can pride yourself on this: You are a girl who never misses a meal, not for madness, not for a man. At least there is that. You can eat. You can drink. You must drink. *Ippon kudasai.* Drink the first beer fast, fast, fast. Now another, faster. This is what you have taught the children for years. How words pile up, how *fast* becomes *faster*, how faster becomes by virtue of the logic of a trajectory we call time, *fastest*, pushing forward, in a sentence, in an afternoon, in your head. *Fast, faster, fastest.* Your small sliver of knowledge is shrinking, your one percent about to disappear. You have forgotten the *ramen* in your rush to drink that beer. Order. Eat. Go slow. Slow time down. Consider time. Consider the future. Steer clear of the past. Forget the future. Think only of this *ramen*. And lists. Lists could save you. A list of what's here. The beer remaining in front of you. The promise of a hotel room at 4 o'clock. The bath you might take at the *sentō* later tonight, the steam inside that will rise, the cold air outside that will wake you afterward. Watch the time. *Is it time?* Leave the *ramen* shop. Go back to the park. Lie down on a bench near the Tourist Hotel. Imagine how cool the room will be, how dark and quiet it will be. Imagine space as an antidote to time. From the outside, how does it look? As if you are sick and tired? From the inside, it's the same: you *are* sick and tired. You are moving slowly now, your head moving in slow motion like the bodies of the women who move at the baths. You are drowsy and full. Consider what you have to do: Get up from the bench. Move toward the hotel. You will move slowly like the fat man you will watch at the airport in just a few days, a man with too much luggage, unsightly bags bursting at their seams. *You're not gonna make that plane, fat man, so just give it up.* You will have too much luggage yourself by then. You are a woman bursting at her seams. Two women at the airport will help you, pulling your bags beside you as you move through the crowd. For years afterward, you will want to thank these two women, these strangers and their kindness. But for now, you have only to get to the hotel. The Tourist Hotel. You wish you were a tourist. Someone with no history here. Someone passing through. Someone who has gone to the castle, watched the tea ceremony, visited the Suzuki School. You know you must be a sight for sore eyes, a woman in love, a *gaijin* sleeping, unable to get up from a bench. Keep your eyes closed. Your mind turned off. Do not think about Nozaki. Do not think. Do not think about what surrounds you. The children who will be coming home from school some time soon, swimming through the heat, staring at you who has fallen asleep. What will the children think? What will they do? Dance past you to get to their after-school schools, their *juku* and their private conversation schools, their schools decorated with moons and stars and flying fish and phrases in simple, practical English? *How are you? I'm feeling blue. When is your birthday? My birthday is today!* You can make a rabbit for the moon. And a cow. Because the cow jumped over the moon, too. Dream of rabbits and cows and men living in construction paper moons, dream of making these things tomorrow afternoon. You have too much time, as they say, but it's not time on your hands. It's time on your *head*, time sitting right smack dab in the middle of your mind, a fat man in a beanbag chair who, once settled, refuses to leave. Get *up*, you fat fucker! Keep your eyes closed so they won't see. Remember, that's how children think, that if you close your eyes, you disappear. Remember, in fifteen minutes you will be alone in a room. As cool as a cucumber, dark as a cave. Remember, a few days from now, you will be gone — poof! — you will disappear out of sight.

Such a magic trick, you can't imagine. On the plane, the woman next to you will tell you not to worry, that if you want to, you will remember it all. The woman behind you will blow her nose again and again, saying, thank God she is leaving Japan, because her allergies are killing her. *Killing her, killing her, killing her, killing her.* What is the name of that fish that people will risk dying to eat at least once in their life? The fish that will kill if it is not prepared just right? The tragedy of bad timing will kill you every time. Try to remember the name of that fish —

In the hotel room, I sleep for the remaining hours of the afternoon, grateful for the anonymity of a brown-and-tan room. When I wake, the beer has worn off and the *ramen* has worn off and the sleep has worn off and I am frantic once again and ravenous, too. I do what I have come to always do, what I would, if I stayed in Japan, spend the rest of my life resorting to: I call Nozaki, remembering that he has said he did not want the last time we saw each other to be the last. When I reach him he tells me he has a client right then and is busy and then he puts me on hold and I wait for him to get back on, believing, really believing he will. As I wait, I can see clearly how absurd I have become, a parody of a woman in love, always calling the man, always waiting for him to return, always believing earnestly that he wants to return. But seeing is not feeling. Recognizing absurdity does nothing to cure the one who's so absurd. I hang up, vowing never to call him again. But my obsessive streak will continue and I will continue calling him in a series of phone booths from here to Tokyo before getting onto a plane. I will pull out my ten-yen coins and dial his number and let it ring for full five-minute stretches at a time, hearing the voices of the *New Horizons* textbook chanting in my head. *Do you have any ten-yen coins, Ken? Yes, I do. No, I don't. Do you have any ten-yen coins? Yes, I do. No, I don't.*

But from here on out, Nozaki won't answer. So this is the last time I hear his voice on the phone. It is clear and familiar and distant and cool, the voice of politeness, of propriety, the enemy of intimacy, which makes me wish for anything, even a touch of anger, which is to say, a touch of love.

Pineapples. Rooftops. Jubilation. Dawn. When I call Amir from the darkness of the anonymous hotel room, he isn't home but his roommate says Amir has left a message to meet me the following night at 7 o'clock.

I consider calling the professor but can't imagine how that conversation would go or what I would do if he found a way to come.

It's final, then, and there's some comfort in knowing: Tonight I am very much alone. And I fall asleep once again, and wake once again as restless as ever, the rhythms of this crack-up with its peaks and valleys and never-ending curves coming each time as a fresh surprise. I try writing in a notebook, arbitrarily copying down words from my dictionary, words I still think I might have reason to use and this, more than anything, is what moves me later on: this earnest belief in the power of words, something tender that I'm not sure I have anymore or ever will again. *Tadashii.* Proper. *Tadayō.* Drift about. Float. *Taeru.* Endure. *Tahōmen-no.* Many-sided. *Tanrei-na.* Graceful. Elegant. Handsome. Fair. I could be taking notes to describe how things might have gone. *Taibōseikatsu.* A life of austerity. Or what will occur. *Taidō.* Quickening. Fetal movement. *Todoroki.* A roar. A throbbing. A beating. In these lists, a story I can't quite hear.

But writing won't keep me. Words won't keep me still. I put the pen and paper down, get dressed and leave the hotel to go out into the night, which is an ordinary night just as it has been an ordinary day.

I wander around in the streets of my borrowed hometown, walking by the *sentō* where I'd been with Shūko and Keiko just a few weeks before and past McDonald's with its garish *katakana* letters in neon lights and toward the black-crow Matsumoto castle with its long-necked white ducks floating in the shallow moat. I want, really want, to pull myself together but don't know how. I wish for Quaaludes or some other drug I've heard about but never tried. I wish for something to wipe the mind clean. Then I'm in front of a movie theater and the signs are pulling me in and it occurs to me that a movie is the one distraction I haven't recently tried.

At the theater, I convince the ticket taker to let me see the last fifteen minutes of *Sister Act*, the only English-language movie in town right now. It's something the ticket taker does not want to do. *Only fifteen minutes left, Miss, do you understand?* he says. I offer to pay full price. *I'd be happy to pay whatever you want*, I say, but he refuses to take my money, saying, *fifteen minutes, Miss, what is it worth?*

The theater is dark and dank and much bigger than it needs to be. I have never seen the seats more than one-third full. Tonight the place is empty. I take a seat in the back and on the side, wondering if this will work, if I will be able to sit still for even the last fifteen minutes of a film. The movie is nearly through. Whoopi Goldberg has been found out by her fellow nuns, only by now, no one cares that she used to be a prostitute. After all, the woman can sing! *Boy*, can she sing! I have arrived in time to see the chorus of women whooping it up in praise of Jesus, in celebration of God, or so the words suggest, though to my mind, it's a celebration of song itself.

This is when something happens, something I can only describe as a fever breaking, a restlessness finally coming to a halt. The scene continues. The women on the screen continue to sing. And there is something about the big screen and seeing all those women, women who look so similar, all of them in nuns' habits, and all of them different, all of them bigger than anyone here in Japan, all of them different sizes, and all of them singing, belting out these huge gospel songs, and they're all swaying, too, moving together and separately, pulled by some collective and primal and internal beat. And then there is the sound itself, so familiar in this unfamiliar place, a sound so big and loud and unapologetic and bold—something hits me. The sound takes hold. I start to cry. Hard, then harder. And with that crying, a sequence of ordinary gestures begins, irrevocable gestures on the backdrop of the night. It is these gestures that save the night from incoherence, these gestures that restore the order for the night, these gestures that divide one half of a life from another in a nearly perfect split.

I will leave the theater. Buy some flowers. Return to the street filled with neon lights. In three days I will get on a plane. Leave this city, this country, these men.

Outside the theater, the air feels cool. Night has taken the edge off the heat. There is still a touch of humidity in the air, but the air is fresh, filled with soft mist. I understand everything now and am glad for the coolness of this particular summer night. I walk with the confidence of the saved. Everything has slowed down, settled into calm. It is as if someone just pulled me from a dark and dangerous ditch, as if by some miracle the world opened wide enough to let me sneak back in.

I walk past the covered shops and over the bridge near the center of town, toward the neon lights of the red-light district, drawn to a certain all-night flower shop. It is a shop catering to salarymen out drinking late at hostess bars. The shop is small, as small as those rooms where medieval mystics lived. I order a dozen long-stemmed red roses for my friend Chieko, who is meeting me for coffee tomorrow morning, and a dozen more for me, knowing I will have them at my hotel for only one night. I wish I had money to buy more. More roses for everyone. More roses to celebrate the night.

I make a mental note to remember the particulars so that later, remembering will be a way to bless the night. Remember the images of this fleeting and floating world. Remember the woman, cross-eyed and young. Remember her posture, straight and calm. Remember that she's dressed in a plaid shirt and jeans. Remember her gestures. How she moves. The way her hands flutter and move. The way she brushes clippings off the counter with a sweep of a palm. The way she pushes fragments of stems and leaves and red petals to the floor, then gives her fat gray cat on the counter a push too, all in one fluid motion before tackling the task at hand: cutting the flowers, and wrapping them, and handing them to me, two neatly organized bouquets of twenty-four roses, roses I pay for, then cradle and carry away in my arms.

Remember leaving the shop, leaving the shopkeeper, too. People are always coming and going, after all. I am no different. Remember this, the fullness of what came next: going out again into that crazy neon street where, without thinking, I looked up at the unwalled sky, breathed in the coolness of this particular night's air, and thought, I'm glad to be here, glad to be unattached, glad to be awake and untethered and floating through this foreign street. Glad for the moment I have nowhere else to go. Glad for the moment I have no one else to be.

At Tokyo's Narita airport two women saw me struggling with two overstuffed bags and helped me shove them along to the front of a line, where, waiting for the line to move, all the movies I had ever seen collided to convince me that still he was coming, that Nozaki would, in a dramatic last-minute cinematic scene, show up just to see me, just to say goodbye.

When a security officer at the gate asked, after noting that I was missing some stamp or another in my passport, whether I had plans to return — Did I plan to return to Japan soon? — I began to cry but answered honestly.

No, I did not. *I do not have any plans to return anytime soon.*

On the plane I sat next to a woman with a scarf around her head. I figured she'd had chemotherapy recently and I fell asleep before the plane even took off, exhausted from weeks of craziness and turmoil when it seemed impossible to rest. When I woke, I realized the woman was a priest, not a cancer victim, and we started talking about what we had each been doing in Japan and why we were leaving and what we now thought. The woman was Swedish but had relocated now to the United States. As a Buddhist, she'd long wanted to visit Japan and finally, for a few weeks, had had the chance. In her time there, she discovered that Japan was all about drama. Even eating, she said, was a theatrical and breathtaking act.

She asked me what I had been doing and I told her about my drama, about Nozaki, and about how my love had been too hard, too needy, that I'd wanted too much too fast. I knew that what I said might sound unpopular, that my friends back home would urge me not to be so hard on myself, that it was wrong for the woman to take all the blame. And it was, after all, something ordinary that had happened to me: I had fallen in love and things hadn't worked out. But I also knew what no one else could: that my wanting had been bigger than anything Nozaki could solve, that my desire had been an insatiable beast, something out of control, a hungry house guest who eats and eats. I told this woman that I didn't know how to describe exactly what happened at the end but it was something like having been out of control, feeling as if I'd leaned too far over some strange and dangerous and invisible ledge and now, there was no way around it, I felt saved. Transformed.

She listened and told me about Buddhism, its two levels of existence, and so forth, and she said I may have visited that second state for a short time.

I told her that I didn't want to forget but I didn't tell her what it was I didn't want to forget. She nodded and said if I wanted to remember, I would. Then a simple gesture followed. She took my arm and pressed her fingers to my flesh.

You've been impressed, she said. *Literally, impressed.*

By the time the plane landed and I had crossed that lonesome ocean and moved as so many do these days, it seemed very strange to me, this simple act of moving from the heavy rain of an Asian island to the heat of an American desert in mid-July.

I had done what was expected. Stuck with a plan. Come home to my nest of family and friends, come home to the familiar Wasatch Mountains over my head.

In Utah, my skin hurt, the air was dry and my nose bled.

In my head I remained very far away.

My people took me on small treks, the tonic of one trip an attempt to cure the last. They treated me gently, though they did not know exactly what had gone so wrong. Travel had stunned me. They could see that much.

I was stunned. A woman, stunned.

One weekend my sisters took me east to see the bones, remnants of dinosaurs that roamed the earth more years ago than I could comprehend. We looked at the bones and marveled at their size. We went hiking to look at petroglyphs, wondering what they might mean. Grocery lists? Cartoons? Lyric poetry? Or love letters to a place? I appreciated the mystery. I appreciated symbols I could not grasp. This trip served as a cold compress for my feverish state: temporary in its relief but a relief nonetheless.

Friends drove me to Wendover to gamble at midday, the casino a dark cave, the lights of the slot machines like *pachinko* parlors I'd left behind. The white-white of the salt flats burned. We barreled along a highway part-real, part-mirage. Fugue country, I thought. The white-white an offense.

My body had stopped bleeding by then, stopped acting as it had so predictably for so many years. I fantasized that something was growing inside, something small and fierce, maybe something that would become a small, fierce girl. In fact my body had simply done what so many bodies do. Shut down after the trauma of travel. Decided on its own to rebel.

On the way home from Wendover, I curled up in the back seat, the vinyl of the car's interior cool to my cheek, the scruffy quality of those sandals I'd spent so much on so long ago now invisible in the car's dark. My friends spoke in whispers so as not to wake me up. I dreamed of where we'd been. Wendover, Wendover. I repeated it in my mind again and again.

I wondered when this would be over, when this would end. I wondered if. If I had stayed in Japan? If I had spoken better Japanese? If I were not so needy? Not so much me?

For a long time, everything I encountered threw me back: I'd take a bath and long for an afternoon at the *sentō*. I'd see children and think of the black-haired children I'd left, wishing myself back to the ABC School.

Cutting up construction paper stars.

Looking for the rabbit in the moon.

Seeing him.

Not seeing him.

I wrote letters, each on delicate white paper in strong black ink. *Imagine you are a dying man*, I'd begin. That the words were cliché never dawned on me. Grief doesn't give a damn about eloquence or anything else.

I never finished the letters, never mailed a single one. Instead I found myself at parties where university people spoke casually about living abroad, how they had had such great times overseas living in Prague or Tokyo or Paris or Madrid and how they couldn't wait to go back because wasn't travel great, didn't travel make you broad-minded?

I stood on the outskirts of these conversations, listening and remaining very, very still, unable to articulate what I was thinking, which was not so simple even to myself, and then someone would ask me what I had been doing before I came here and I would answer that I'd been living in a small city in central Japan, and questions would follow, natural ones: *How was it? What was it like?* And I would want to say that those weren't the right questions, that it had all been very complicated for me, difficult to summarize, impossible to translate because those years I lived in Japan seemed nothing less than real at the time, not some hiatus from a more important or more compelling life, but in the end I had had to leave that life behind and doing so felt terrible, like suffering a small death.

Instead I would smile as best I could and say the beer was good or it was more quiet there than here.

The last time I saw the professor I gave him a bouquet of dried roses that months before some students who had visited me had offered as a gift and I intended to tell the professor that I wanted him to have those flowers because the flowers were one present that, in their delicate state, I couldn't ship, and also because the goodness of those boys had always reminded me of him. But somehow I never got around to saying that. Instead we spoke awkwardly of very little if anything at all. And I noticed his rectangular glasses and his polyester suit, the kind men of my father's generation wore, and I looked down at his shoes, the little metal chains across the front, and wondered how I'd ever become involved with a man who wore such shoes, and then, when I had become so mean.

When I said good-bye to Amir, I cried and cried, and he kept saying, *no tears, no cry*. He said he was afraid he hadn't been good to me, that he'd found me very interesting but perhaps I'd found him not so interesting in return. I shook my head to say no, that wasn't true, but couldn't think of how to translate what I really wanted to say. I wanted to say many things. That Amir had been interesting to Marilyn-san. That he had taken care of me at a most peculiar time. That the way he had taken care reminded me of how my boy cat used to take care of my new girl kitty, licking the girl cat, cleaning her, getting the knots out of her neck, loving her in an ordinary and beautiful and bodily way, saving her from herself, from going to seed.

I had often wished I could tell Nozaki more about Amir and pass along to one man those things I had learned from the other. For does not love, like science and philosophy and art travel, always in a circular path? Buddhism came to Japan from China through Korea. The French Impressionist painters who were so strongly influenced by Japanese woodblock artists learned of Japanese woodblock techniques only accidentally, through the throw-away prints that dishes, which were exported from Japan to Europe, were wrapped in, prints which, like newspaper, cradled the dishes so the dishes in transit would not break. And wasn't it only by accident that the first Europeans set foot in Japan? The Portuguese were on their way to Macao, I'm told, when a contrary wind drove them ashore. It was then that they landed on a small island off the coast of Kyushu.

I wanted to tell Nozaki about Amir and Amir, now, about what was becoming clear: that all gifts are borrowed, then passed along in good faith to someone you hold dear.

In the end, as we sat there on a bench at the train station, I borrowed a word from Nozaki, one he had earlier used with me. *You've been* tokubetsu na *to me*, I told Amir. *Special.* Because he was.

Two days later, I saw Amir one last time by accident. I had spent the afternoon with my friend, Rachel, and was walking her to the train station at the end of the day. Then, right before us, coming out of the crowd, emerged Amir, taller than anyone else, a large figure who loomed overhead. Rachel receded into the background as good friends will do and Amir and I talked for a minute, asking each other, *What are YOU doing here?* Then he took my hand and kissed it and walked backward into the moving crowd.

So here is my final image of Amir: a man disappearing like a mime exiting the stage, Amir shrinking, getting smaller and smaller with every step away, Amir smiling, his right hand above his head, Amir waving, and before disappearing, Amir raising his hand, blowing an imaginary kiss.

The last time I tried to see Nozaki it was raining hard after a night of violent storms. I had asked a taxi driver to make one small stop and when he did, I jumped out of the taxi and ran up the block to Nozaki's place, and unhooked the rope of Nozaki's blue gate. That small, blue plastic umbrella — I felt compelled to return it. Not to seemed to invite bad luck. Also, I had some books in translation and CDs that I wanted to leave. I rang the bell. Twice. Three times. Then I did something that remains one of those small but regrettable gestures that I cringe every time I think of it, nearly a decade later. I tried the door.

The door was locked that day. I don't know if normally it would have been or not. But it was locked that day and so I left my gifts and that blue umbrella in a plastic bag, which I hung on the door.

Then I ran back toward the taxi just as the driver came running up toward me.

Take care, take care, the taxi driver said, raising a red umbrella over both of our heads, the two of us running in synch as quickly as we could.

We arrived at the taxi breathless and drenched, the rain having blown its way under the umbrella, the rain having soaked us, despite his care.

Sitting in the taxi, running my fingers through dripping wet hair, I thought, *OK, this is it,* and I wondered, is this how Nozaki felt the other night? Exhausted and unhappy but also finally, resigned? I was resigned. I was leaving. *Netai. Dekinai.* I wanted to sleep. I wanted to die.

The windshield wipers flashed in double time. The taxi driver's white gloves shone. It was raining cats and dogs as they say, and I wondered, why cats, why dogs? Why not fish? Why not goats?

Slouched over in the back seat, I remembered something I'd seen on television years before: that when cars were first invented, the windshields shattered at the slightest speed. A chemist dropped a test tube on the floor one day and—by accident—unwittingly discovered the material necessary to make windshields sturdy, nearly shatter-proof. An accident of good fortune. Something practical borne from an innocuous mistake.

A bad storm, the driver said, our car crawling through the narrow streets. The windshield wipers ticked away like a fast-paced metronome. I breathed in and breathed out and listened to the rain and looked at the tile-roofed houses in pale blue and gray.

For the rest of the ride, the driver remained silent and I was grateful for this. I was also grateful that he'd brought me that red umbrella in such a small but dramatic gesture of concern. Doesn't every story end this way? With the heroine going home? And some small gesture of goodwill on a stranger's part?

I closed my eyes, wondering if maybe it didn't matter who took care of you in the end, only that someone tried.

And when I opened them we had arrived at the train station in Matsumoto, where the taxi driver helped me maneuver my bags and where the rains continued. And the memory of that huge rain is something that stays with me still, as does the image of a midget woman in a yellow pantsuit I saw from the corner of my eye, also getting out of a taxi that day, an image of the small juxtaposing itself against the largeness of the sky like a surreal version of a Japanese landscape painting.

In Tokyo I spent my remaining hours wandering the streets and drinking whatever I could get my hands on and standing once more at a lime green phone booth, listening to the phone ring again and again. When I hung up the phone, a stranger touched me on the shoulder and asked in perfectly polite but worried English, *Are you OK, Miss, are you OK?* and I shook my head but found that I was crying too hard to form the word no.

Who DID this? he asked.

Finally, finding my voice, *No one,* I said.

What happened? he pressed. It was still raining hard, hard, hard. It felt as if it had been raining forever, as if the rain would continue, too, for a very long time. Neither of us had an umbrella. Both of us were getting drenched.

Nothing, I said to this stranger, the last to make a gesture of goodwill. Shō ga nai. *Really. Nothing. It can't be helped.*

And because it was true, because nothing *had* happened, nothing I could translate into words at any rate, and because certain things in your life, the most important perhaps, cannot be helped, the answer made me more sad than I will ever have words to explain.

As time went on, I adjusted slowly. And as I adjusted, I would be glad for physical reminders of the place I'd left behind. Those blue dishes. A book of poetry from a certain man. A string of teeny-weeny *origami* birds.

Some seventh grade girls folded the birds for me and put them on a string as a good-bye gift. When they honored me, I remembered the story from our *New Horizons* textbook about a little girl in Hiroshima who tried to fold a thousand cranes before dying, and I wondered how far she got or if that story was true.

Thank you, I told the girls. *I will cherish the gift always.*

To never forget, they said. *Please remember.*

The string of birds would hang on the doorknobs to different rooms for many years to come, and sometimes, as I opened and closed the doors, paper birds would fly off, one at a time, little pieces of carefully folded colored paper littering the dark wood floors of various apartments that I tried, each time, to turn into homes. I saved them, picking up the flyaway birds and putting them away in a box — the gesture of someone who wanted to hold onto what she could.

he men in my country are long gone now. I live in Iowa, a square and sturdy place. I like where I live, like how quiet the town is, lots of students and professors spending a good deal of time in their heads. I like Midwestern stoicism, which reminds me of the Japanese reticence toward anything but the smallest of talk. I like the weather. I like talking about the weather, like observing shifts in season every year.

In the springtime in Iowa, when a long winter has passed and the sweat of summer is still to come, the cornfields enveloping the countryside look like Japanese stone gardens, as if Buddha has taken a finger and drawn circles into Iowa's deep dark soil. I like spring here, how the entire state blossoms and blooms. I like the fullness of a lush green rush. Since I come from a desert, this seasonal celebration still seems strange and new.

I like how in the spring you can walk right past a honeysuckle bush and the scent will be sweeter just a few yards past.

I like how in the summer shopkeepers on the pedestrian mall come out with their hoses each morning to spray familiar red brick-lined streets and people mow their lawns and I walk to town to get coffee and take it all in, the sight of these clean new streets and the smell of freshly cut grass, which is something I lived without for a few years. Without that absence I would never notice the fullness now.

In autumn a new batch of students arrive in sloppy sweatshirts and faded Levi's and their presence transforms the college town as only young people can, filling up the streets and the bars and the coffee shops and classrooms with wonderful noise, making this place new all over again. I walk to and from campus, grateful to know the trees: the sugar maple on Burlington, the small ginkgo in front of the library. At the end of fall, the ginkgo loses its bright yellow leaves, its perfectly constructed little fans, as if it has taken an oath, and the leaves fall and arrange themselves becomingly on the sidewalk's gray slate.

I like walking home in winter, making my way from the university where I teach, through a small city park near my house. In that park there is a phone booth on the corner of College and Dodge where people, young women and middle-aged men, some of them speaking softly and some with great animation, make calls at all hours of the day and night. I can't help but wonder who they're calling and what kind of dramas are unfolding and whether or not they will, these people who are strangers to me, be able to fold themselves back up once the dramas are through. And I can't help but wonder which of these people, like me, have felt that they are waiting, forever waiting, for an answer that never comes.

I have an apartment here I can afford and love. The apartment is like all the apartments of my past. High ceilings. Hardwood floors. But it also manages to feel entirely new. I like renting now, which implies a passing through. I understand the blessings of this apartment's views.

Here I am surrounded by windows on three sides.

Here I am enveloped by trees and light.

Here I live simply, as if I were perched on top of a very comfortable branch, living inside an elegant birdhouse.

And there is a certain view in my birdhouse that I happen to like the best. From my couch in the living room I can see the bedroom from a slant. A slice of the bed. Half of a window. A small strip of the wall. A still life. Furniture as fruit. Maybe to see a room indirectly is to see a room at its best. Maybe to see on the sly is to see something complete.

In the bedroom I have placed a single red paper umbrella in a corner near my bed. In the living room on a backdrop of plain white walls hang two rectangular strips of dark green rice paper, plain and pure; they remind me of Mark Rothko paintings and how contradictions work, how something can be both subtle and clear, large and intimate, arresting and absent.

On a table in the living room there is a glazed red ceramic bowl too large for a single portion of rice but too small to hold more than an orange or two. In it, I have mixed up petals from bouquets of flowers past: orchids from my mother for my birthday one year; yellow roses from Ellen as a graduation gift; leaves from many bundles of red tulips, which I buy regularly at the co-op and watch as the petals hold tight for a few days, then fall outward all at once, a spray of swimmers falling back in voluptuous unison into the clear water of a vase.

I gather up these petals and these leaves and I put them in the glazed red bowl and note how they dry, shrinking and changing but never quite losing the beauty they once had as they become, in time, something else instead.

Is it possible to live a good life alone? Is there such a thing? I don't know how to answer except to say that there are days now, as I'm folding laundry or watering the herbs or washing the dishes or listening to my mother's voice on the phone and suddenly I am caught off guard with a feeling so full, so overwhelming and so stunning, that I cannot imagine there is a word in any language to take it all in. I stop. Everything in me stops. I am not alone. I am surrounded by much — laundry and dishes and the herbs growing on the windowsill and my mother telling me on the phone to *just snip the babies off the overgrown spider plant and put the babies in water and the babies will sprout* and at these times I see: Plenty surrounds and embraces me.

Love is wide, Nozaki said. With the arrogance of youth, I thought I knew what he meant. How love was open and generous and kind and full. But now I know that love is sometimes narrow too. This is the paradox. Perfect but flawed. Like the handmade paper I learned to make in Iowa. Something that seems fragile at first touch but whose essence is very, very strong.

I dream sometimes of traveling again. I like the sound of certain places. Of Tanzania. Of Prague. Of Belize. Of Brazil. Of home. Or moving home to the mountains. To the smell of sage. To my mother's backyard with its tomatoes and mule deer and scrub oak trees. The scrub oak leaf—the most beautiful in the world.

The other day I heard a racket outside and went out my kitchen door to stand on the building's rooftop, which doubles as make-shift porch, a place I like retreating to to see what the weather is doing or to take a break from writing this book.

Looking past the angles of my neighbors' rooftops, all straight lines and triangles in rusty reds and whites and shades of green and brown, I could see where the noise was coming from: hundreds of black crows clustered in a hickory tree. The sight was so stunning, I knocked on my neighbor's door so she too could see.

It was almost evening. The crows created a stark silhouette, their bulky bodies black and bold against a darkening blue sky, their wings flapping as if they were leaves, fallen, then risen, dead but now come back to life. I asked my neighbor if she thought the crows were coming or going and she said she thought crows were a species that stayed put year round. We continued watching and we both kept quiet for a while and I was trying to remember the word for a seasonal feeling.

Kisetsukan, the Japanese would say.

My neighbor reminded me that this tree where the crows now clustered had, the summer before, been hit by lightning in a terrible storm. The lightning in that storm had split the hickory's trunk straight in half, and we had wondered at the time what would happen, if the tree would survive or die. That the crows now chose this tree, my neighbor said, was a sign.

A sign of what? I asked.

That the tree would be just fine.

Sometimes when I think of Japan, of *my* Japan and the woman I was, I think of something that happened back before I left — something that reminds me that stories begin before they begin.

It was a night before winter turned to spring and I was seeing someone, a man fluent in many languages. I thought he was smart and elegant and I liked him because he liked me, he said, because I had a very distinctive nose and I liked him, too, because he was a man of two worlds and once, when I was sick with a cold, he left two presents in front of my door: a small bottle of antibiotics and a clove of garlic, objects from the new world and old.

We met at a party on the previous New Year's eve. There had been a blue moon that night and I had thought of blue moons as unusual, though I've since learned they are not. I had asked him if he liked country songs because I did, because I loved them all, songs by Hank Williams and Patsy Cline and Willie Nelson and Emmylou Harris, songs that seemed sweet and simple on the surface but were much much more, songs about the layers of nostalgia and the strains of restlessness we all feel or will, songs about looking back and moving on, and love and rage and forgiveness in all its forms. And when he had said yes — that that's how he'd learned English, by listening to the radio and practicing to those sad slow country songs — I had taken his answer as a sign because in those days, I was always looking for signs. Maybe still, even now, I'm looking for signs.

After the party, he had walked me to my car and asked if I'd like to have tea some time. Maybe he had liked the sound of my voice, the clarity of it, or maybe I reminded him of someone in his past, someone he'd once known. To me he seemed entirely new, like no one I had ever met or even imagined meeting before.

A war was about to begin. *There will be losses*, the president of the United States would say. And he was right. There were. The war would shatter the lives of thousands of people. But those people, those losses, they seemed very far away. And here at home, people celebrated the war by wrapping yellow ribbons around the thick waists of trees. It was a confusing time. Maybe all times are. But on this particular night, there was no war to think about yet. The trees were bare of the perversity of ribbons; there was nothing but the sweet clear promise of days ahead.

Tea? he had asked that first night as we stood out on the street, after the party, that icy cold night. I knew that he meant did I want to have tea with him some time in the near future, not immediately, not right then.

Sure, I had said. *What about tonight?* It would be a shame, I thought, to waste the night of a blue moon.

So we drank tea and peeled oranges and talked as we sat on my small black couch, my blue-eyed boy cat curled up and sleeping between our feet, my button-eyed girl cat jumping from one lap to the other, then settling down between us, a cloud of calico bliss, and I knew that this was the perfect way to start the new year, watching the blue moon go down and the sun come up, drinking tea and eating oranges with a man from a country very far away, a man who wanted to be with my animals and me. The man stroked the girl cat on top of her cottonball head till the girl cat drooled and the boy cat nearby purred in his sleep and the man told me he liked my kooky cats and the oranges on this night, they tasted especially good.

They're shaped like little boats, I had said, swinging half-moon slices in the air and rocking them into the shore of my mouth. I wondered how long the man would stay, if maybe he'd stick around for breakfast and what the cats then would think about that.

For now the cats murmured from their slit-eyed states, dreaming of birds in the backyard, of travel and adventure, of feathers and tender flesh. And when the last slice of the orange had sailed, the man had picked up the rinds and ate the skin as happily as he had the flesh, and I smiled at the fact he showed no shame toward his hunger and

I wondered what the peelings tasted like when you ate them like that, whole.

After that, we took to walking sometimes late at night in the streets of my neighborhood and one night, on one of those walks, the one that reminds me of the whole of Japan, I asked this man questions, what kind of words he missed, what kinds of words refused to translate into English from his native tongue.

I remember the night clearly and can conjure the scene. But when I do, I confess that it seems different than I imagine it felt at the time — wider, richer. As if it happened to someone other than ordinary me.

The woman walked with the man she loved arm-in-arm down a quiet tree-lined street, past white frame houses that looked desolate to him, all that space surrounding them, all those porches, empty now of anything but swings, and past sturdy brick bungalows that she called charming, all those yellow-lit windows and the promise of happy chaos inside, mothers chopping onions in the kitchen, fathers scolding children, saying *Stop that jumping on the bed!* Can't you just *smell* dinner cooking? Can't you just *see* the boys playing rough-house on that bed? She kissed the shoulder of the man's brown winter coat and imagined what they looked like to people watching from the comfort of inside: a happy couple walking arm-in-arm down a quiet little tree-lined street.

The man looked up at the night sky and he thought about her question, trying to remember certain words that did not translate, words that did not sound quite right in English, in this, his borrowed tongue.

He stared straight ahead and without slowing his pace began to speak.

I miss, he said, *the word that combines happiness and sadness and irony all in one.*

Bittersweet? she asked.

Close, he said, *but it lacks the intensity I'm talking about, the fullness.*

He told her the word as they continued to walk and she smiled at the sound of it, a word so pretty, it sounded like a song. She made him repeat it again and again, wanting very much to hold on to it, believing, really believing, if she tried hard enough, she could.

Many years later, when they had both moved on, when everyone had moved on as people these days are wont to do, she would not remember the word, would not remember the man's face, would not remember anything except the feeling.

The feeling.

No fanfare. Just that.

That she would remember.

She remembers that still.

Acknowledgments

For support that made the writing of this book possible, I want to thank the editors of literary magazines who published my work as well as the Rona Jaffe Foundation; the Corporation of Yaddo; the Ragdale Foundation; the Utah Arts Council; Writers@Work; the University of Iowa; Saint Mary's College of California (the best place on the planet to work); and Neeti Madan at Sterling Lord Literistic, Inc. (the most gracious of agents).

During the writing of this book, I carried around with me a slip of paper with something that Amiri Baraki wrote in a review of Billie Holiday: "Nothing was more perfect than she was. Nor more willing to fail." Those words comforted me. But it is the people who provide enduring solace.

I want to thank my teachers: Ted Conover, Carol de St. Victor, Paul Diehl, Linda Hogan, Patricia Foster, Pam Houston, William Kittredge, Susan Lohafer, James Alan McPherson, Honor Moore, Marilynne Robinson, Bob Schacochis, and Terry Tempest Williams.

Providing sustenance in many forms over many years were friends and colleagues, including: Shūko Abe, Richard Adams, Dan Albu, Annette Aldous, Mary Allen, Doug Balli, Jackie Berger, Kate Birch, Joe Blair, Barbara Bryan, Jody Panto Chong, Steve and Frances D'Andrea, Mary Dickson, Elizabeth Dietz, Meredith Field, Michael Gardner, David Hamilton, Greg Heffron, Ai Ito, Elaine Jarvik, Eric Jones, Mildred Keller, Laura Kelley, Elmar Leuth, Maggie Lyman, Amy Margolis, Keiko Matsuda, Martha McFarland, Christi Merrill, Michele Morano, Holly Mullen, Takako Nagahara, Laurel Nakadate, Dee NaQuin, Suellen Novotny, Sue O'Hara, Rene Paez, Mackenzie Pitcarin, Don Porter, John Price, Dana Pridham, Marcelyn Ritchie, Leslie Roberts, Margaret Rostkowski, Mark Saal, Carol Severino, Ravi Shankar, Noriko Shirahata, Jess Shoemaker, Kathy Stall, Amy

Stewart, Lynne Tempest, Mary Trachsel, Kris Vervaecke, Rachel Walker, Bridget and Hiroaki Watanabe, Susan Whitney, and Vanessa Zimmer.

Ann Bauer, Judy Copeland, Yiyun Li, and Chieko Mimura read drafts of this book in manuscript form and provided insights for which I am grateful.

Carol Houck Smith and her vision came along at a crucial time.

Jo Ann Beard was constant, Ellen Fagg saintly (and sardonic and everything else anyone could want in a best friend).

To Carl Klaus, teacher, editor, and friend—what do people do without a Carl Klaus in their lives?

Holly Carver, Andy Douglas, Sara T. Sauers, and Charlotte Wright were wonderful; I remain in awe of the University of Iowa Press, which cares about one thing: publishing beautiful and intelligent books.

And to my family—my parents, in particular—thank you for the reminder that the deepest pleasure of travel, indeed its very ache, has been and will always be returning home.

sightline books . . . .
The Iowa Series in Literary Nonfiction

The Men in My Country

MARILYN ABILDSKOV

Shadow Girl: A Memoir of Attachment

DEB ABRAMSON

Embalming Mom: Essays in Life

JANET BURROWAY

Fauna and Flora, Earth and Sky: Brushes with Nature's Wisdom

TRUDY DITTMAR

Essays of Elia

CHARLES LAMB

The Body of Brooklyn

DAVID LAZAR

No Such Country: Essays toward Home

ELMAR LUETH

Currency of the Heart: A Year of Investing, Death, Work, and Coins

DONALD R. NICHOLS

Memoirs of a Revolutionary

VICTOR SERGE

The Harvard Black Rock Forest

GEORGE W. S. TROW

Made in the USA
Las Vegas, NV
23 December 2020